The Autobiography of
A. ~~Nobody~~
Somebody

A.Somebody

Copyright © 2012 A. Somebody

All rights reserved.

ISBN-10: 1478395486
ISBN-13: 978-1478395485

DEDICATION

Everybody is *A.Somebody*!

This autobiography is dedicated to all the *Somebodies* out there because it is not only celebrities who have interesting lives. Unknown people also have fascinating stories to tell and I invite the reader to follow my example and produce their own book in a similar way, thus making a neverending series where *Nobodies* have a literary outlet under the title:-

'The Autobiography of A.Somebody'

LEGAL NOTICE

Printed in the United Kingdom

The author has asserted his right under the Copyright, Designs and Patents Act, to be identified as the author of this work and the owner of the intellectual property right of any book produced using or under the title of 'The Autobiography of A.Somebody.'

This book is sold subject to the condition that it may be lent or circulated without the publisher's and author's prior consent, but shall not be, by way of trade or otherwise, resold, hired-out, or circulated for financial gain without the publisher's and author's consent in any form of binding or cover.

The scanning, uploading, and distribution of this book via the Internet or any other means without the permission of the publisher or author is illegal and punishable by law. Please purchase only authorised electronic editions, and do not participate-in or encourage piracy of copyright materials.

Your support of the author's rights is appreciated.

Although this is a summary of the author's life, parts can be considered fictitious as one should never let the facts get in the way of a good story. It is not the author's intention to offend or discredit individuals or corporations, and this shall act as advance warning that should a company or individual decide that there is a case to instigate legal proceedings they should be aware of the well known legal principal *'the man of straw'* and an apology is the only form of recompense available to them.

ACKNOWLEDGEMENTS

There are many people who have inspired me in bringing this book to publication.

A few individuals stand out amongst the many friends who have encouraged me to write about some of my *funny* life experiences. Clive Panto, because he was right about *that* chapter as well as everything else. Chris France, for making me believe that I could write a book. Andy Rawcliffe, who did more than was expected. Dawn Howard, for stopping many potentially litigious comments. My brother-in-law Phil, for allowing me to write about *the* most traumatic moment in his life. Chris Witts and David Lowdell, who championed me in fulfilling one of my professional goals and Viv Frost, for her finishing touch.

Finally and most importantly to my wife Helen, who has supported me through every stupid idea I have ever had.

CONTENTS

QUOTE

CHAPTERS

1. THE CÔTE D'AZUR
2. TAKE-OFF
3. GOOD TEETH REQUIRED
4. FOR BETTER FOR WORSE
5. TINY FEET
6. MY LONDON
7. JUDGE AND JURY
8. BLACK BELT
9. SQUARE PEG, ROUND HOLE
10. LE MANOIR
11. THE CHANGE
12. AU REVOIR ENGLAND
13. BRICKS AND MORTAR
14. COPS AND ROBBERS
15. RICHES TO RAGS
16. THE RELUCTANT GUARDIAN
17. JE NE COMPRENDS PAS
18. FRENCH PLUMBING
19. THE CAP FITS

SHOPDROPPING

ABOUT THE AUTHOR

The late Malcolm McLaren once said:-

"It is better to be a flamboyant failure than a benign success."

Perhaps I have been waiting all my life for such a quote to justify the path I have chosen.

CHAPTER 1
THE CÔTE D'AZUR

Today is my Birthday!

I am 49, slim, reasonably fit and healthy, with blue eyes and silver-peppered hair. Helen, my lovely wife, sings *Happy Birthday* as she hands me a freshly baked croissant adorned with a single, flickering candle. I am sitting in my house in the South of France with no career, no prospects of a career and riding a financial roller-coaster. I have tried several new ventures, all with limited success. However, I am happier than I have ever been.

A birthday is a snapshot in time and as I reach my near half-century I reflect on the words of Aristotle who said: *"Although we must have goals it is often the journey that is more interesting than the goal itself."* With this in mind I think about life and the journey's ultimate end, which is death. Not a morbid thought, but certainly the conclusion to all our stories one day.

My story is this autobiography - a history of my being and a platform for personal clarity. Perhaps it will strike a chord with those who have made similar choices to me and for those who have not, it may inspire (or deter!) them to follow in my footsteps, if only for a short while, until finding their own path.

I worked for British Airways man and boy, I have also been a management consultant, a magistrate, a hotelier and a website entrepreneur. I have spoken on the radio and appeared on television, as well as having had articles written about my life in the national newspapers.

Not rich enough to be retired and still too full of beans, Helen and I are taking a break from the *day job* - renovating our pretty villa, our fourth in eight years.

The morning air is already warm and crickets sing their songs from hidden auditoriums in the bushes as the sun illuminates the full detail and majesty of the distant mountains. A startling blue sky mirrors the azure of the Mediterranean.

We drink in the view, whilst enjoying the perfume of lavenders and flowers as bees buzz around and birds swoop in and out of the olive trees. We inhale the air like wine connoisseurs to revel in the aromas.....

"What is that bloody awful smell – is that you?" Helen says as her face contorts with disgust.

"Bugger all to do with me, it must be the dog!" I snap back.

The smell gets stronger and overwhelms the bouquet from the flowers.

"It must be that bloody septic tank playing up again." I say knowing that tomorrow morning my hand will be down the toilet, unblocking the U-bend, otherwise we really will be in the *merde*!

Paradise lost, or at least temporarily suspended, we decide

to make an early start and head off for my birthday lunch. Although the journey is longer compared to the motorway, today we will enjoy taking our time as we drive along the dramatic coastal road.

We come across a GB plated convertible, driven by a wannabee Grace with her passenger Cary, wide-eyed with fear at the dizzying drop appearing at every hairpin bend, already terrorized by the locals' *laissez-faire* attitude to the Highway Code – it was just like this in *To Catch A Thief!* After five years we, however, are now hardy motorists and are exhilarated by the staggering scene laid out before us.

Arriving at the beach restaurant I am greeted by cheers from smiling friends who have all been sworn to secrecy about our *romantic* lunch *à deux!* Helen gives me a cheeky grin and I am more than happy to forgive her duplicity.

So many delicious delights are brought to the table that I hardly have room for the cake – should have passed on the birthday croissant!

I look around the table and think what a lucky guy I am to be in this place, in this moment, having started out as just another *nobody*. I have followed my own way and had great times and interesting adventures. Meeting Helen gave us both the wings to really fly and make a new life. We now have so many unusual friends, of different nationalities, from different walks of life and all with fascinating stories of their own to tell.

Late afternoon arrives and with laughing goodbyes ringing in our ears, we finally set off back home. Tomorrow will be another bright spring day and the sun will shine for many months through the heat of July and August, then further on into autumn when November's monsoon-like rainfall will confirm the change in season.

We have not moved here for the summer months; I always believe that an English summer, remembered as a child, can never be bettered. It is the *shoulder seasons* with warm bright days and cold nights that make late lunch on the beach such a thrill, especially after having returned from a morning's skiing in the mountains. This area is labelled as the *Alpes Maritimes* and it does exactly what it says on the tin!

Our finances will be stretched to the end of the year, when hopefully work on the house will be finished. We will then decide whether to sell and search for another renovation project or rent the villa out for the summer season, giving people the opportunity to experience our lovely home for their precious two weeks holiday.

We have chosen an unconventional way of earning a living, but it allows us to stay in France and be masters of our own destiny. This is never going to get us on the *Sunday Times Rich List*, but our view of success is not measured in monetary terms; it is measured in terms of freedom and in the life enhancing experience of living in a beautiful part of the world, which has the essence of paradise.

But I digress. I'm going to start my story by telling you how it all changed - for the better or for the worse. I'd like to think for the better....

CHAPTER 2
TAKE-OFF

Cops and robbers was always a favourite game with me and my two brothers as we ran around the house, trampolining off the sofa and launching across the living room in hot pursuit of each other. This rowdy behaviour usually resulted in something being broken and nine times out of ten my parents seemed to know that I was the culprit behind the boisterous game. Overly-rough fights saw one of us, usually me, chastised by a parent.

"That's enough!" my mother would scream as she pulled us apart. *"Look what you've done to the sofa! Right, that's it, I'm calling the naughty boys' home. Go and get your coat and wait in the porch for them to come and collect you!"*

Minutes felt like hours as I stood looking through the porch window in my duffle coat waiting for the collection van. Somehow I always managed to make an apology seconds before they arrived.

"I'm sorry Mum. I won't do it again."

"OK. You had better come back in. I will have to call the naughty boys' home and cancel that van." She said as she ruffled my tousled mop. Replacing the receiver she said: *"That was lucky, they were just coming up the road."*

Maybe the saying is true – *"Give me the child until he is seven and I will show you the man."* My character was already taking me on a different path to my siblings who were more cautious like my father, whereas *I* had inherited my mother's curiosity, cheeky charm and self-belief. She always said that it didn't matter what I did in life as I would always come up smelling of roses.

Schooling was never my thing and I would question why I had to learn certain subjects such as spelling. A quango education board trialled the ridiculous theory that children would learn faster by writing phonetically, thus words such as *'eny'* and *'enuf'* have left a lasting mark into adulthood. When I write in a hurry, almost as a dyslexic, I am unable to see my *errers*.

At the age of thirteen I had the opportunity to leave my comprehensive school for one year and go to a boarding school set deep in the beautiful countryside of Surrey. They took one boy and one girl from every school in the county, selected because they felt they would suit the style of education at Tilford. I was desperate to go as even at this young age I was bored with mainstream education and wanted something different. I loved that year of independence and the encouragement we were given at the boarding school to develop our own ideas and characters, but on returning to my old comp I found it hard to settle down and could not wait to leave. I wanted to travel, get out into the world and have adventures.

I decided the best way to feed my pioneering spirit was to work for an airline and use the cheap travel offered as an employee perk. I applied to British Airways and was successful in joining the I.T. department, where I would spend the next eighteen years climbing the corporate ladder. In the early days all I wanted was adventure, ready cash and hopefully, even-readier stewardesses. Within the first week of getting my staff travel perk I was on a plane, off to somewhere – anywhere.

Everywhere!

These were heady days for a nineteen year old and during my many trips to the States I developed a passion for classic American sports cars. I finally found my favourite one through the local papers, a 1967 Pontiac Firebird. She was bright red with a curvy body, shiny chrome grill and enormous wheels. A throaty rumble from the 5.7 litre engine announced her arrival when I returned home late at night, much to the annoyance of my parents. She was an expensive mistress and I kept three jobs going to keep her filled with fuel. I was working for British Airways during the day, had a bar job at night and every weekend was spent at the Inns of Court in London, working for a barristers' chambers, setting up their computer systems. I worked like a dog but she was worth every penny.

Any car in a teenager's mind is considered as a *babe magnet,* but girlfriends could never compete with my American dream girl.

"When are you going to take me somewhere nice instead of just driving me around in that bloody car?" asked my latest girlfriend on the phone.

"But I need to buy a new carburettor fuel jet because it's not firing fuel into the piston pots." I replied in a voice as if talking to a mechanic. *"Once it's fixed then we can go out."*

"I'm sick of it – you'll have to decide. It's me or the car."

A long silence followed as I considered my options.

"Errr... can I get back to you on that?" Suddenly the line went dead.

Although I loved the car, even I could see that this was a one-sided relationship. All I had to show for my endless hours of work was a sexy sports car that spent most of the time parked outside my office waiting for me to finish work.

I wanted something lasting to show for all my hard graft, to own something that gave me independence from my parents and freedom to do what I *wanted* when I *wanted*. I finally said goodbye to my American beauty and put the money from the sale towards a deposit on a house. Although others may have considered me as irresponsible and immature, even then I had enough foresight to see that I could do better in life. Getting on the property ladder early might help me climb out of suburbia to somewhere more interesting. With a large mortgage, I typified the saying *house rich penny poor,* but I managed to make ends meet by working excessive overtime and by renting out the spare bedrooms of the terraced house.

Two good things came out of this drudgery. One was that I always had a ready means of escape, travelling the world at every spare opportunity on a miniscule budget with my cheap tickets. Many of my friends were crew and they often smuggled me into hotels in exotic faraway places. My adventures sometimes took me on a crazy whirlwind schedule as I hopped on whatever flights were available at the time - San Francisco on Friday, Cincinnati on Saturday and Hawaii on the way home!

Youth and drive gave me the energy to beat the jetlag, shrug off the shift work and maintain a well-run house. The second benefit was that it taught me to multi-task and to have no fear of hard work. These qualities did not go unnoticed by my senior managers and after a couple of years, I was promoted to a senior mainframe operator.

Once, following a particularly tiring shift, probably not helped by my Washington weekend, I somehow managed to grind the airport to a complete halt by deleting a programme that allocated stands to aircraft. This was a major incident and would cost the airline greatly in lost revenue as planes were displaced globally and needed to be rescheduled. This *slip* would take a complete day for the situation to be resolved, but at least it got me noticed! Even in a crisis, I seem able to keep a cool head and although it was *me* who had created the mess, it was also *me* who put it right. Ironically, my error helped me move on into a more managerial role – or maybe they just wanted to get me out of the way!

Thereafter, I was promoted to various positions, all within the I.T. arena. As this was a growing and vital part of the airline my skills were very much in demand and I capitalised on them, eventually taking charge of the data networks and then desktop purchasing contracts. My particular skill was the ability to understand the technical jargon of the I.T. nerds and then translate it into simple terms to keep the wheels of the supply chain turning. When working at the barristers' chambers I was exposed to legal terminology and developed an inherent understanding of this *second foreign language.* Such a niche skill made me the perfect candidate for the role of Supply Chain and Contracts Manager.

Over the years I worked alongside many external management consultants and without wanting to sound bigheaded, I found that I had a far greater knowledge than all of them. This gave me the confidence to eventually leave the airline and freelance as a management consultant myself, working on lucrative contracts for, amongst others - Network Rail, the Metropolitan Police, the Financial Services Authority, EDS and finally the Greater London Authority.

Even though I had some interesting times and a certain amount of professional success, I always felt that I was in the wrong career but I didn't know what to do when I finally grew up – I still don't!

CHAPTER 3
GOOD TEETH REQUIRED

As a young man I had the sort of sexual desire that is driven by hormones and controlled by embarrassment. I was able to engage girls as friends as I could always make them giggle but never enough to laugh their knickers off! As women get older they say that a guy with a good sense of humour (GSOH) is the quality desired by most women, but when younger, these same women always dated the sulky guy, all edgy and rebellious. Funny how in a young man moodiness is sexy, but in an old man it is just grumpy.

I was never what you might call 'a manly man.' I had the sort of boyish good looks (I am told) that encouraged nightclub bouncers to reject me at the door with comments of, "*Not tonight sonny*," with no further explanation given. It was often a way of flexing their muscle and little attempt was made by me to change the situation. I was not prepared to try to convince the Neanderthal at the door that he had made the wrong decision; besides I was never really a nightclub sort of a person. I was not able to dance unless fuelled with alcopops and a success rate with women was dented by my ability, or lack of, to consume booze in volume.

After a few serious relationships, I found myself in my late twenties back on the singles market. With a lack of female colleagues in my *techie* workplace, it appeared that to meet women, one was forced back into the nightclubs. I felt the club scene was for the younger crowd, but wanted to find a girlfriend in the decreasing number available from those who had not already been paired-off, married or become pregnant, either in or out of marriage. A friend and I discovered what we thought would be a seam of gold in the form of an *Over 25s Divorced, Singles and Separated Club*. We became regulars, then realised that the people there, were single for a reason. Whenever Gloria Gaynor's song '*I will survive*' rang out, it was a call to the dance floor for every bitter woman to stop what she was doing and gather in the centre around their handbags and sing along with venom to the words: "*Go on now go! Walk out the door!*" as arms gestured a former partner to leave.

Some wonderful girlfriends came and went but I knew that they were not the *one*. Those who passed through my life would have made great wives for somebody, just not me. I was happily independent, not commitment phobic as some women accused me of being, and the thought of settling down with someone who *would do* and producing a family was a social pressure that I felt was not my particular calling.

Don't get me wrong, I've always had an easy way with children. When I was growing up, me and my brothers were taken to work by our mother who was a health visitor. If she couldn't find a babysitter during the school holidays she would drag us along to help weigh the babies at the clinic and be on hand to play with the other children whilst she made her rounds.

A few girlfriends had children of their own and this served

as a trial to fatherhood. Knowing that I was not the natural father of the child meant that the bond was never strong enough to make a break-up hard. It reinforced my notion that perhaps life had more to offer me than parenthood and maybe I would meet somebody who wanted to share my vision of eternal marriage without the obligatory addition of kids. We could find a different way of fulfilling our lives.

Whilst living as a bachelor in a funky one-bedroom flat in West London, life seemed to be passing me by. Work was all-consuming and with 24-hour shifts, working on the computer network systems at the airport, I was isolated from day-to-day life and more importantly, the weekend party scene. A brief, but very passionate affair with a married woman added an element of excitement for a time, but I always knew I was her way of shaking up a mundane existence of being a wife and mother. I was very happy to be her *play thing* if only for a short while. I would often say *yes* to people if they asked if I had a wife…….. but she was not *my* wife, I would add with a naughty smile.

With my thirties just around the corner, single women were becoming thin on the ground. My neighbour and friend was an airline pilot, who with his braided shirt and captain's hat, made me convinced he would be great bait to all the alluring stewardesses. However, he was one of life's *nice guys* and never capitalised on his *uniform* appeal. So unassuming was he, that the day he qualified as a commercial pilot, he wandered around Tesco's in his work attire whilst buying food for the weekend and was approached by an elderly lady thinking he was part of the shop's security team!

Weekends would be spent as two single guys with good jobs and smart apartments, sitting watching mindless television programmes. But after another beer and biryani Saturday night-in, I decided that we needed to try a new approach and place adverts in the local newspaper's lonely hearts column - a dating process now virtually non-existent thanks to the internet.

I may have drunk slightly more than my friend as he was unconvinced of my plan. After a few more drinks, I rang the number advertised and my advert appeared the following week - alcohol does have a funny way of changing your priorities.

Single Guy.
Late Twenties. Blue Eyes.
Fair Hair. Slim. GSOH
Looking for fun lady
with good teeth.

After a few days, I rang the message box with anticipation. I was surprised to hear that I had indeed received four enquiries, all of whom claimed to be in possession of nice gnashers. In response to the first lady caller, I set a date for a few days hence and waited with excitement as the day itself approached. Being a modern man I had arranged for my date to collect me from my apartment. My phone rang and on answering, my panic stricken friend screamed:

"I've just seen your date! For fuck's sake don't open the door. Pretend you're out."

The doorbell rang and a soft Scottish voice came over the intercom:

"Helloooo, this is Audrey."

"Hi, come in."

I quickly explained to my friend that it was too late, she was already here and it would be callous to ignore her now she'd made the effort to turn up.

"*Good luck mate,*" he laughed.

When she reached the door to my apartment I opened it with trepidation. There stood Audrey, all 4½ft of her, both tall and wide. She did indeed have nice teeth - individually - but with relative ease you could shove a pencil between each one!

The evening in the local pub passed with reasonable conversation. In need of a lift home, I left it until we were driving up my road and politely excused myself from a second date. Audrey puckered up in preparation for her goodbye kiss but all I could think of was a *lipsticked* Ken Dodd!

The other dates came and went. I took each one to the same Chinese restaurant on consecutive nights and was pleased that the waiter made no comment other than,

"Good evening Sir. I am delighted to see you again after such a long time."

Lonely hearts dating was not for me so I withdrew my advertisement with haste. I believe that when physical chemistry is forced, with high expectations from all concerned, natural attraction cannot develop - or if you want the honest truth, none of my dates were shaggable!

After the horsey ladies' dating disaster, I started to ask myself what I was really looking for in my ideal partner. I reflected on past lovers and what attracted me to them in the first place. All former girlfriends had special elements about them. Some were a learning curve of emotion and physical adventure, yet all had the similarity of being very attractive and stylish. They always had an attitude and a personality that made them confident and interesting; this added a dimension to their sexual allure. I am always curious as to how their lives turned out, not because of any desire to rekindle old flames, but surely it is only natural to reflect on past lovers and what could have been.....

Sexual appeal in a future girlfriend was essential, but so was a shared sense of morals. She had to have a thirst for life and the strength of character to take that life by the scruff of the neck. The ability to cook the odd meal every now and again would be lovely - but never mind - you will hear about my wife later.

One final thing, good teeth required!

CHAPTER 4

FOR BETTER FOR WORSE

It is my 32nd birthday and I am in a pub celebrating with a few friends. I have only drunk a couple of beers but this is enough to make me feel tipsy and brave. I see a very attractive blonde across the bar and decide that I would like to meet her. I walk straight over, introduce myself and then spend the rest of the evening chatting to a very confident woman with whom I just *click*. Numbers are exchanged and a future date arranged – this means I have pulled! What a great birthday.

After a couple of dates with Helen, I invite her to my apartment for dinner; I want to impress her with my cooking. She likes healthy eating so I decide to show off with a meal including as many vegetables as I can cram onto a plate. Freshly squeezed fruit and vegetable juices will also be on offer next to a bottle of fine wine. I have all day to prepare a romantic dinner for two so decide to resurrect the juicing machine from the back of the kitchen cupboard and try out a few concoctions before she arrives.

The juicer minces and squeezes any item put through its blades and after each mix is ejaculated from the spout, I test a glass of the highly fibrous soup. Throughout the day I sample and drink several pints so by the time Helen arrives I have consumed every fruit and vegetable known to man in fluid form.

As conversation flows I feel my tummy start to grumble and expand. The brewery within super-inflates my stomach to such a degree that my shirt stretches so tightly there is a danger of a button bursting off and taking her eye out.

Like a simmering pan of thick soup my stomach starts to complain. *Flob-a-lob-a-lob.*

"You feeling alright?" Helen asks as I sit sweating from my brow.

"Yes. Just a bit off colour." - *Flob-a-lob-a-lob.* - *"Will you excuse me?"* - *Flob-a-lob-a-lob.*

I rush to the toilet in the hallway and only just make it in time as my world collapses through my backside. Many trips to the toilet are necessary as our romantic date descends into an embarrassing evening of smells and noises from a bathroom which is now my haven and will be for many hours as I moan and groan, fart and shit myself into oblivion. Not the best start to our relationship! Thankfully Helen saw the funny side of my misfortune and realised my intentions were well meant.

More time spent with Helen makes me realise that she is a unique individual and I soon realised that I had found the *one* - somebody to walk with me on the adventurous path that is life. She has a great sense of humour but there is sadness in her history. She is a very positive person but has yet to fully expand on her family situation. She mentioned that her parents died several years earlier but it was obvious that she was not comfortable enough with me yet to really open up.

As the months pass Helen talks more about her childhood and her parents and how great it would have been for me to have met them. She talks in such a positive manner that I'm beginning to think they are actually still alive. Maybe I misunderstood?

"I know, I have to go to Cheshire next week for business, why don't we both go and visit Mum and Dad?"

I agree and never question the fact that I thought they had died years earlier. I obviously have it wrong.

We arrive at a small cemetery on the outskirts of Knutsford and walk through the quiet graveyard. I say nothing. We stop at two gravestones and Helen kneels down and replaces the old plants with flowers whilst talking casually to the slabs of granite. I stand and listen to a full blown one way conversation thinking all the time that this feels a little weird – but at least I can now confirm that they are dead.

"Mum, Dad, I would like you to meet the new man in my life." She turns and looks at me.

I am caught off guard in my daydream state and now feel awkward and embarrassed, but politely say:-

"*Hello Mr Jeremy. Hello Mrs Jeremy,*" as I nod at each grave.

"You silly sod." She laughs. But I realise that for her this is a significant moment.

Having met the parents I am invited to meet her brother Phil who lives in the South of France. First I make sure that he really is alive! He and his current wife had been models for many years but decided to escape the rain of Manchester and set up home in sunnier climes. We land at Nice airport and as we walk though *Arrivals* we see the trio of Phil, his wife Sue and their son Alexander, who as a six year old is obsessed with dressing as Robin Hood - with bow and arrow never far away. We wave and walk towards them and from only a few feet away, *Robin* takes aim with a rubber-suckered stick making a direct strike to my testicles.

"Fuck!" I scream as I double over in pain holding my groin.

"You O.K.?" asks Phil.

"Yes. No damage done." I grimace, realising my dirty weekend is off the cards.

We leave the airport in Phil's car and he drives like a madman. Being a very poor passenger who gets car-sick on the shortest of trips, I am unsure if I will make the thirty minute journey before vomiting. We arrive at their house, Phil having taken every corner like a racing driver and I fall out of the car, green in the face from the hair-raising trip and sore in the groin from bruised testicles. As we have arrived late we decide to call it a night and chat more in the morning.

I have been asleep for less than five minutes when Helen shakes me from my slumber.

"Are you awake?"

"I am now you've woken me."

"There's a mosquito in the room and it keeps biting me. Will you do

me a favour and kill it?"

I turn on the light, stand naked on the bed and leap around like a trampoline artist, trying to smash the mosquito with a shoe as it dances around the ceiling. The bed suddenly collapses beneath me and causes lamps and bedside tables to fall over. With the noise of crashing, shoe smacking and shouting, Phil bursts into the room

"What the hell is going on?"

I am standing on top of the wrecked bed with a shoe in my hand, naked and exhibiting my hugely swollen testicles. Helen passes me a tissue and I hang this over my genitals. I cannot think of anything to say other than *"Please excuse my modesty."* To this day, I still don't know what the hell that means!

Much laughter the following morning concerning the evening's events relaxes us all and we instantly feel at home in each other's company. We talk a lot about Helen and Phil's family and the good times they, their sister and their parents had together. I am flattered when they say that it is a great shame I had not met their mum and dad, as they would have loved me. However, what they tell me next is so shocking and sad that I am rocked in my boots.

Phil talks about his first marriage to a lovely girl called Jane and the joyous occasion of their wedding day. But six weeks after their marriage he came home to find her brutally murdered, in an event so violent that thirty years later, on the anniversary of her death, he is still deeply affected. A cloud of sadness descends over him and little can be done by his current wife except to be around - her presence alone is often the only support that can be given.

Helen and Phil continue with the story of how their family sorrow was further compounded three months later by the death of their grandmother who was a front-seat passenger in their mother's car when a horse, ridden by a young girl, bolted and landed on the bonnet, crashing through the windscreen, leaving their grandmother dead, their mother blinded and Phil, who was in the back, the task of leaning over the bodies to steer the car until it naturally came to a stop. A few months later, their previously healthy father died of a very aggressive cancer, followed shortly after by the death of their mother, her cancer probably accelerated by grief. Needless to say, Phil and Helen are unusual characters who carry great heartache, yet remain positive about life, despite unimaginable sadness.

As time passes, I realise Helen's complex character and my own individuality attracts and entwines us more and more. We cannot believe that in the *whole world* we have managed to find each other. We start living together and our marriage follows two years later. With Helen's parents long since deceased, and my own mother having passed some years earlier from cancer, the only financial help available for our wedding was from my father. Without pushing too hard to confirm how much he might be donating to this happy occasion, there soon came the realisation that his contribution would do little more than cover the entertaining of the friends *he* had invited, leaving all other expenses to be met by us. However, this did not stop my father and soon to be step-mother regally welcoming our guests at the wedding reception.

Our wedding was arranged for a beautiful Friday afternoon

at St Anne's Church on Kew Green, followed by a reception at Strawberry Hill House, a Georgian Gothic castle used by Mick Jagger to celebrate his 50th birthday. The wedding was a joyous occasion at which I spent most of the ceremony crying with happiness alongside a bride who was passing me tissues and telling me to *pull myself together* – but I knew we shared the same joy and desire to spend the rest of our lives as one. A wedding is a happy occasion but can also be very poignant as we remember those loved ones who cannot be there to witness our big day. For me and especially Helen this added to the charged emotion of the moment.

Phil gave his sister 'away' and so he features heavily in our wedding photos. Each time the shutter clicked he struck the perfect pose – easy when you've been a model. The album reveals him looking like a film star while I've gone more for the startled rabbit look.

The early part of our marriage was bathed in the hazy glow of romance. But after several years little habits - once seen as cute and quirky - can start to irritate and annoy. Helen's inability to cook or operate a washing machine or any electrical item in the house, due to having little interest, means the majority of domestic chores, apart from cleaning, are left in my hands. What I don't give her credit for is her ability to redesign the house and get her hands dirty in doing it which keeps us moving from one place to the next to make money; is also allows us to be in the position of having a choice between the rat race and freedom.

As a relationship matures and differences are accepted, amended or ignored, the realisation dawns that marriage takes effort; one must be content with one's own being, then happy with your partner and then marriage itself. Getting married later in life has meant that we have the maturity to deal with upsets and difficulties. It is important to recognise that being apart - if only for a few hours - makes for a stronger bond as ultimately we are all still individuals and it is healthy for us to have our own space sometimes. A colleague once revealed to me that since her husband had retired she was annoyed at how he was getting 'under her feet'. His constant 'being' during the day was resolved when she reminded him that she had married him for love, not for lunch. They took up their own interests again and he became a member of the local golf club, a haven for many and so the balance was restored.

Married for fifteen years at the time of writing, we have dealt with our ups and downs in a grown-up manner - at least I like to think so, but this may not be my wife's opinion of my sulking! We spend an enormous amount of time together, and for us, it works. We have flipped the roles in our house and I am the one who cooks and sorts the washing, whereas she does the chores generally associated with husbands. At a recent *Dry Stone Wall Building Course,* the men did not expect such a feminine woman to be up to her neck in mud and lumping large stones around with an enthusiasm unseen before by the instructor. He asked me if I was going to offer assistance as she moaned and groaned, lifting large rocks into place. My response was that I was better off leaving her to her own devices, as over the years I've come to realise that her beautiful looks belie a tomboy at heart, always better in the company of men than of women, as she has more interest in these types of activities than those of the kitchen.

I love Helen dearly but I don't tell her this often, as the inordinate amount of time we spend together makes me forget and become less appreciative of her. We have found our level whereby we can laugh, work and play together yet still enjoy each other's company, to the point that we each feel a little bit lost when apart.

CHAPTER 5
TINY FEET

After several years of marriage the issue of the patter of tiny feet is discussed, and rejected by me as nonsense.

"But I want for nothing else in life," sobs Helen from the bathtub.

"I just want to love and be loved," she continues in between tears.

Now, I have heard the 'never wanting anything again' as the reasoning behind many a pair of shoes, but this is different. The tiny feet commitment? What about our freedom and how will we cope with early mornings?

Eventually, I can take no more of the long, sorrowful face around the house.

"OK," I concede, *"go and get the bloody dog then!"*

Screams of delight echo through the house, and within seconds a list of breeders is produced. Much planning has obviously taken place already and many discussions with friends behind my back as a breed has already been chosen. It is with great delight that we find a pack of West Highland White Terrier puppies, only days old, and so we rush down to Kent to select our new family member. We choose a ball of fluff amongst the tangle of tails. When we return four weeks later, we find our little *ball of fluff* has snowballed into an enormous puppy, obviously the dominant one of the litter and now twice the size of her siblings. One of her kennel names is Charlotte, but we decide that Charlie would be more appropriate for our little tomboy.

We load her carefully into the car and make the long journey home, with Helen cooing all the way. Many weeks pass; each morning I come down to the kitchen and open the door to the spare room to be greeted by a smell and mess only puppies can produce. I am at the end of my tether as every day we clean the room before going to work with me moaning about how the dog needs to go back. Just at the stage when I cannot take the mess any longer it suddenly all stops and we have a house-trained dog.

Over the years, she has provided us with great joy. She is our baby and fills any void that may be there due to not having children. We walk her twice a day whatever the weather, and for Helen, who worked from home, she provided great company and structure to her day. A white ball of fluff, Charlie has never lost that puppy look and has a personality that matches many of the women I have dated: strong, different and slightly odd, but in a cute way.

At the end of every day, we take Charlie onto the front lawn and wait for her to have a last pee before bedtime. To keep an eye on her, I use a torch and shine it in her general vicinity. Since puppyhood, she has seen this beam of light as a game when it hits the ground, so tries to chase and play with it. Seeing how amusing this is to her, we start taking her into the cul-de-sac and buy a torch with the power of one thousand candles! I stand at one end of the street as she chases the light beam the length of the street and back again. After several mad runs, with her tail tucked between her legs and ears pinned back as she runs at break-neck speed trying to catch the light, we realise this does nothing but pump her up before bedtime. We soon regret what started as fun, but is now an obsession with a dog who whines all evening once the sun has set, wanting the torch to come out and play. Any sighting of the torch sees hours of whining and grumbling, leading to shouts from us as we struggle to watch television of an evening. Although now fifteen, she has never lost the thrill of chasing *torchy* and we even have to be careful with reflective surfaces which create a light beam such as a watch face or a wine glass.

Charlie looks like a teddy bear and is often mistaken for a puppy, but what people don't realise is that she is the Daughter of Satan and teeth are soon shown to any vet trying to come near. For all their years of experience, many have admitted defeat and a muzzle is the only means of control as the low growls start. People in the waiting room can hear what sounds like a large aggressive dog and double-takes are common when we trot her out of the surgery.

Hanging out of the car window with ears flapping in the wind she is a contented soul, barking at passing dogs and their owners, happy in the fact that she's travelling faster than them, so in dog language she can verbally abuse all she sees - like a white van driver shouting lewd comments at a pretty girl!

Despite being senior, Charlie is still very active, and has an eye for large male dogs, acting like a teenager who has just spotted their idol, squealing with delight. People comment that they have never heard a dog be *so* vocal, and obviously we have come to recognise the various squeaks, growls and rumbles and their meanings. We know when thunder and rain is on the way as she prowls and barks anxiously; we definitely know when it has arrived. But for all her irritations she has given us lots of fun and love over the years and we will be devastated the day she is no longer here. As I write this book, she is sitting at my feet snoring loudly, but I know that after her power nap she will be up and running around, grumbling and squeaking for a walk.

CHAPTER 6
MY LONDON

After a restless sleep because of the Sunday night blues, I rise at 6:30a.m, drag my sloping shoulders down the corridor from the bedroom to the bathroom and turn on the light after I close the door, so as not to wake Helen. I raise my face to the mirror to look at the dark rings around my eyes and at the pale complexion we, in England, suffer from for nine months of the year. It's as if I'm staring into my very soul *"Who the fuck are you?"* I ask my bewildered self.

I have bathed and shaved the evening before to buy me a few minutes extra in the morning. Today I will be at the station on time and be ready to start the pushing and shoving of the train and tube with extra energy. I brush my teeth and run my fingers through my hair which will quickly be blown in the wind of the trains to a style I am unable to recreate however hard I try. I think of my life and the milestones I have achieved, or failed and hope that someday it will all make sense.

I am first on the train, having stood at the exact point on the platform where I *know* the train door will appear. It stops right in front of me and I push the button and step on with confidence ahead of the other cattle muttering behind me. I see the seat next to a coughing man and make my way in haste to ensure people entering the train from the other end of the carriage do not get there first. I sit down and open the *Daily Mail*, chosen not for its content, but for its size as it is smaller than the broadsheets - those papers that make your arms longer and impose into your neighbour's space. I sit and breathe ever so slowly and with minimum depth as the man next to me coughs and sneezes in my direction. If I don't inhale so deeply perhaps I will avoid getting his chesty cough?

I hold my newspaper high above my brow to make sure I don't make eye contact with the pregnant woman who has just entered our carriage. At least I think she is pregnant. I don't want to make the same error as last week, by offering my seat to a young girl who I thought was blessed with child, when in fact she was bloated with chocolate and chips. There is a quiet sigh of relief that somebody else has volunteered, almost press-ganged, into vacating their seat, so now we can all relax again until the next station.

Becoming engrossed in your daily newspaper is a ritual and once I have read the articles repeated from the night before, I start working on the crossword which disengages me further from the rest of the people in the airless bubble. Doodling around the edge of the crossword, I decide that my general state of tiredness does not allow me sufficient concentration to continue, so I lighten my mood by staring out of the window at the passing houses next to the train tracks. They offer perfectly habitable accommodation provided your nerves can stand the regular rumble of a train as it shakes the interior like a timetabled earthquake. However, according to local estate agents these are *fantastically convenient for all transport links.*

At the next station, our day drops a few more notches. A bloody busker has just got on the train.

"Morning Ladies and Gentlemen. Let's put the smile back on your faces with a few sing-a-long songs." he says as he strums the battered guitar in preparation for his howling.

He starts with that well known cheery ditty by Leonard Cohen

"Suzanne takes you dow-ow-own to her place by the ri-i-i-ver....."

None of us are inclined to sing along. He finishes his shortened version and then walks around with his hand outstretched. No money is given to this X-Factor reject and as he leaves the carriage he shouts:

"You can all fuck off, you miserable tight bastards!"

What a nice chap I think to myself.

The palette across London is grey, a certain shade of grey I hadn't noticed until revitalised by a recent holiday. The only colour punching the air are the motorway signs in blue that I can see from the bridge as we cross the busy motorway.

I want to get in and out of the office on time. I have an important meeting. I am important! I have told those people we met on holiday how important I am in my job. I have swallowed the self-importance pill every day and I have status, both at work and in my local neighbourhood. I have taken the tablet so often that I am buoyed-up with a new title that makes people think I am more important than I really am.

We arrive on time at Waterloo station and hurry to exit the train like the busy people we all are. This sea of grey, black and blue suits is punctuated by the odd flash of colour from a woman who is not restricted to the sombre code of the man's office uniform. Her red jacket makes her bright in the crowd and says she is not afraid to be different; it lightens her face like a movie star and is a refreshing change to the normal business attire. Perhaps she is in marketing, advertising or some other career where she has to be creative, unlike the majority of us shuffling along the platform, hurrying to spend our days pushing paper around desks, waiting for the clock to strike five, going to pointless meetings and day-dreaming our lives away.

I busy up to the ticket inspector who is the all-powerful man filtering people through his exit gate. His wide shoulders are held back not by good posture, but by a massive stomach, pushing him upright, restrained by a large belt holding enormous trousers. Another fat man walks up and they posture, admiring each other. *Is he bigger than me? Is he smaller? Do I look that good?*

We bottleneck to the exit and the smell of damp woollen coats, sweat and garlic-breathed people fills the air. We all try to stand behind the person who is our height as we like to feel the same and if they smell nice we are attracted like bees to a flower.

I pass the ticket inspector with no acknowledgement. We have seen each other several times a week over many years, yet neither of us shows any recognition. I am free. I have passed through the turnstile and my season ticket says that I have regular work in the metropolis of London. I quick-step through the station and pass the many coffee and sandwich bars that litter the area. They create a shopping mall atmosphere to every available large public space, which makes us feel comfortable with our surroundings. I look for the familiar names of the coffee shops and I know that wherever I am in the world, they will be exactly the same. In one way, I like to know my territory, yet in another I am jaded with the repeated brand tedium.

My journey is almost automatic. Passage through the tube gates is quick as we all swipe our little blue cards designed to speed us through the system. A few steps further and I stand on the right of the escalator to allow all those in a hurry to run down the left side, almost tripping with speed. On hearing a possible train approaching the platform, the people standing on the right start to fidget and move into the fast lane or tut and grumble at others in front to move along.

I am on time today, so can expect to see the blind man and his dog as I have done for many months. I stop and watch in fascination at the scene about to unfold. The man steps towards the escalator and at a known point the Labrador stops. The man bends down to pick him up. With dog in arms which is almost half his size, he feels with his foot until it catches the first step of the rapidly moving escalator and slides forward like a man slipping on a banana skin. The perfectly trained and courageous guide dog suddenly turns into an oversized *handbag dog* whimpering and whining the entire descent, but both man and dog know each other's fears and abilities and together they take on the world. My previous offer of assistance with the escalator was met with "*I'm blind, not stupid!*" Perhaps he has been asked one too many times, but I suspect that is not the case as I rarely see others offer assistance to those in need if it is likely to delay their day.

My journey is taking me to Tower Bridge for my role as a management consultant. This is a job undertaken after leaving the airline industry after 18 years and manoeuvring myself into the position of being accepted for redundancy. I was unwilling to step out of the company without a *golden goodbye* as this was to be the financial springboard for me to follow my passion for the law and perhaps retrain as a barrister.

Although I had several happy years at the airline and some great times travelling around the world, I found that ultimately this was not enough to compensate for the monotony of working in I.T. nor stop the chafing of corporate chains.

My exit plan entailed me trying for many months to become the most useless man in the department and therefore a particularly suitable candidate for redundancy. It was the lottery ticket that many wanted to win but it was always some other lucky bastard, not me. My uselessness eventually paid off - I was finally made a very good redundancy offer and my response was instant, despite a sudden feeling of rejection and fear. So here I am. My wish came true and I got my *golden goodbye*.

Be careful what you wish for…

CHAPTER 7
JUDGE AND JURY

Having spent so long complaining about the lack of stimulation in my job at B.A. and wishing to be set free, I had finally achieved my goal and was now a respected management consultant. I didn't want to admit to Helen that I was already disillusioned with my new career. Of course the money was great but I still felt professionally unfulfilled.

There were highlights, however, in the last few years, but these came not from paid employment, but from time in the courtroom – not as a defendant, I may add – but as a juror and later on as a magistrate! Most people think I'm pulling their leg when I tell them that I am a Justice of the Peace. Perhaps a good lesson in *never to judge a book by its cover*. I have experienced this kind of reaction all my life.

Most people 'judge' me based on my cheery boyish looks, my jokiness, a strong London accent, a lack of formal qualifications and my readiness to laugh at myself. Although I don't take myself too seriously, I *am* somebody who thinks deeply about life and cares very much about right and wrong. Some people when they first meet me swipe me away as no one special, but when they get to know me they tell me they're really surprised at the many layers to my character. Why not say it? Why don't we all say it? I am *A.Somebody*. It is this thought process which has led to the title of my autobiography.

One of the big surprises for most people is that I am a JP and this is how I became a magistrate.

Following two jury services, one at my local crown court in Isleworth and the second, at the far more interesting, Old Bailey I discuss with the court clerk how cases come before the jury. The clerk explains that if a person is charged with an offence and not dealt with by way of a Fixed Penalty or caution by the police, then they are summoned before a magistrates' court where one hundred percent of cases start, of which only three per cent end up as trial by judge and jury. The clerk encourages me to do more research and explains I am the perfect age to be recruited as a Justice of the Peace.

I talk at length with Helen about my day in the courtroom and express an interest in becoming a magistrate. The next day she goes to my local court and gets a leaflet and an application form that she leaves on my desk. I devour every detail and after additional research I decide to apply. My application is fast-tracked because of my age (applications from people under thirty-five is rare) and a letter quickly arrives inviting me to interview.

The interviews are gruelling, questioning my morals and beliefs and the ability to make fair judgements. The panel consists of a judge, a barrister, a solicitor and four magistrates and they fire questions at me, ranging from mundane traffic offences to drug abuse, rape and murder. An in-depth discussion on the sentencing of a rapist engages me head-to-head with a female magistrate. After much debate we still disagree and the next question from the judge throws me slightly when asked if I believe if there are any corrupt judges. My response is quick and balanced when I explain that in all levels of society, and whatever position, there will always be an element that works outside of the boundaries laid down and enforced by the law. He raises an eyebrow but gives no indication as to whether I have just shot myself in the foot or not.

During the following months, all records and references are checked. I am then called for a second and much tougher interview at which the Court Chairman questions me aggressively about my maturity and ability to make sound decisions. At the time I had no idea that this harsh scrutiny was because he was extremely eager that I should join the bench; this was why he wanted to test my judgement to the maximum. If appointed, at the tender age of thirty three, I would become one of the youngest magistrates in the UK and therefore he and the other panel members needed to be certain that I was up to the immense responsibility it entailed.

Many months pass before I receive a letter from the Lord Chancellor confirming that my application has been successful. I am invited to attend a civil ceremony at Kingston Crown Court to take the oath and be officially sworn in as a Justice of the Peace.

For this very proud occasion Helen wears black, punctuated by a Guard's Red Jacket. I choose a light green Italian-cut suit, last seen at my wedding a year earlier and prized in the wardrobe as a *special* article of clothing. We arrive at the court and are greeted by a sea of black, navy blue and dark grey suits. Even the relatives of the other soon-to-be magistrates abide by the unwritten sombre dress code, reserved for formal occasions and it is with surprise that I notice even their children are all still a good ten years my senior.

We are divided from our spouses and families and I am sitting on the benches of the courtroom before the presiding judge, the mayor and other dignitaries. I glow like a beacon in my green suit in the ocean of dark attire. My time to approach the judge and take the oath nears as they move alphabetically through the crowd. The black-gowned official looks solemnly at me and calls out my name. I spring to my feet like a jack-in-the box and beaming from ear to ear, almost skip with pride up to the judge (afterwards Helen said that I looked like I was doing my Frank Spencer impression!).

The oath is taken with my hand held high and I bark out my allegiance to the Queen so loudly in the direction of the judge that his wig almost lifts off. This is the proud moment which now allows me to use the title JP at the end of my name.

An official group picture is taken outside the courtroom and is to appear in the local newspaper the following day. Although it is printed in black and white it does little to muffle the brightness of my suit. I am easily recognisable in the wall of earnest expressions - I smile so hard for the photo that I think my face will break.

Once home, I telephone a disinterested father who likens me to a poacher-turned-gamekeeper. Although an unsubstantiated comment as I was no angel when younger, he probably considers that as the cheeky and rebellious one of his three sons, I precariously trod the fine line between right and wrong. Thankfully, growing up in a secure loving home, it meant that like most young men it was little more than high spirits.

My training as a magistrate is to last for several months, arranged as a day here and a day there, which allows me to continue with paid employment as the role is voluntary and unpaid. After many months of training and now partnered with a senior magistrate, who will serve as my mentor for the next year, my time has come to sit on the bench for my first day in court.

I arrive early and am greeted by my mentor who is a very brusque lady in her late fifties. The clerk of the court outlines the day's business and asks for a couple of minutes so she can take her place in the courtroom before we enter. My other colleague for the day is a local councillor - a pompous man who is amused by his own wit, yet unable to recognise others grimacing at his juvenile humour. He is like a butterfly, unable to stay focussed on one conversation and particularly one that does not allow him to show his political knowledge or promote his own opinions. He cares little for his appearance, his posture or the people who voted him in to his position. It is very clear that as the new boy, he regards me with complete disdain.

The hour arrives and we march in a conga of three towards our allocated court. The first person in our line is *The Pompous Politician*; my mentor is acting as senior magistrate and will take the central chair and I follow in last, checking the door is closed behind us.

We enter the courtroom, it falls silent, and then all persons present leap to their feet as we walk to our seats with heads held high. We stand as the clerk of the court, ushers, lawyers, press and other officials bow their heads in respect to the magistrates. The only people not to bow are the defendants who stand staring at the Justices to see if they recognise any from previous appearances. All the court waits until we are seated. This is quickly followed by whispering and shuffling of papers. The usher rises and announces the first case to be heard. My shaking hands open my note book which will be quickly filled with names, times, dates and information. I don't want to miss anything so I write down absolutely everything! I can type quicker than I can write, and with handwriting (and of course spelling) that is akin to a demented ten year old I am praying that my notes are not sent up for judicial review.

The first few cases fly past me as legal process is discussed and people are moved in and out of court. I have written several pages when I notice my colleagues' pens have not even been lifted from the table. Maybe they have forgotten to ask me to keep notes? Good job I'm alert! Or maybe I'm just over enthusiastic.

A short trial takes place concerning a chip shop owner who is charged with assault and battery (yes, honestly!) of his estranged wife inside the restaurant. His plea of not guilty is greeted with silent enthusiasm by his lawyer; he has worked hard on the pre-court papers and will now have the opportunity to display his oratory. As witnesses stand and are asked questions by the crown prosecutor, I write so much that eighteen pages are soon filled with notes to remind me of the important issues to be discussed by me and my colleagues in the retiring room. At the end of the trial, I am still busy writing when my colleagues leap to their feet; the courtroom attendees follow in quick succession and I am left still writing my notes. *The Pompous Politician* glares at me whilst he waits impatiently for me to gather up my papers. Opening the door, my files start to slip apart and fall over the floor. I try to maintain gravitas as I scoop them up and exit the court with my fellow Justices.

As the new boy I am asked to give my opinion first. I must speak about the evidence and give reasons behind my findings. Frankly, my notes are a mess but large stars drawn in the margins allow me to locate what I believe to be the crucial facts. I am concerned that the evidence given by the defendant and the victim are different and believe this to be the hinge on which *Guilty* or *Not Guilty* rests. The words used by the defendant as he struck his estranged wife in front of many customers were:

"Fuck off you bitch – you fucking arse."

Yet he seems to be contradicted by the victim who relays this part of the evidence as:

"Fuck you bitch – I am going to fuck you in the arse."

I highlight this enthusiastically to my colleagues who listen politely but *The Pompous Politician* rolls his eyes as if to say that in his opinion, the only *fucking arse* in the courtroom that day was me............

Several years later and having completed the intense training, I am able to take a more senior role besides sitting in judgement in the adult court. I am also trained to deal with juveniles. My work as a self-employed management consultant means I am flexible with my time and able to attend court on a more regular basis than some of my colleagues. This means that I can deal with the larger cases such as rape, murder and other trials that require several days' court work. The normal sittings required by the Lord Chancellor is one day every two weeks. With my availability I exceed this quota on a regular basis to such a level that he writes to our Court Chairman demanding to know why I am sitting far in excess of his expectations. Perhaps his letter thanking me for my commitment and considerable loss of earnings was lost in the post?

I gain a reputation for being tough but fair. The sight of my poker straight face and adopted mannerism of looking over the top of my glasses like a wise old owl sees a flurry of plea changes; court *hearings* are often shortened to a morning of paper processes and sentencing.

Becoming a magistrate allows entry to a quasi club that is populated by many people who have more contacts than any person could imagine. Their circle encompasses royalty, actors, politicians and poets. I knew that I never really fitted into their social network, and even after several years never made it to the very active dinner-party circuit.

I am always asked for donations to the various charities supported by my colleagues, but never once receive an invitation to the social gatherings it involves. However, there is a glimmer of change when I receive a call from a senior magistrate who tells me about a charity event at which many are expected, and in general conversation I am led to believe that I am indeed to be included.

"Anyway, enough of this chit-chat old chap." he says in an accent reminiscent of an old colonial colonel. *"The reason I'm calling is that we are having a little soirée next Saturday and the usual suspects will be there, along with a few politicians and ambassadors."*

"Oh really!" I reply in an excited voice, already planning my attire for the evening event in my head.

"Yes. But we are a bit short-handed and need somebody to help serve drinks and a few nibbles."

A long silence follows.

"Would you be a decent chap, pop on a dickie bow and help us out?"

I politely decline the request due to another *faux* engagement and he abruptly ends the conversation.

I hang up. *"Tosser!"* I shout at the phone.

After some time, the realisation dawns on me that I am different to many of my fellow Justices. I reflect on why I was first attracted to this very powerful position. I'm doing this because I want to put something back into my community and society. For me and for several of my hard working colleagues it was never about social advancement.

Even though I still loved the court work, it still didn't compensate for my restlessness. Helen, ever the adventurer, was happy to discuss perhaps moving out of London and trying somewhere and something new - maybe to just shake things up a little. Helen could find employment anywhere as an interior designer, but I would need to adapt my *paid* work and make it more portable.

If we were to make a move, I would need to resign from my local court and reapply to another. I decided that having served my *unpaid* civic duty very well over many years, that to coincide with moving, it might be the right time to step down. This was a really difficult decision as I felt I was doing something good for society and that the judiciary needed young blood like me. With a heavy heart, I resigned and a dejected chairman accepted my resignation after trying to convince me to stay; she believed I was one of the most balanced, fair and relevant magistrates on the bench and would be greatly missed. Should I decide to return one day, she told me that the courtroom door would always be open.

I miss the work of the court and many of my wonderful colleagues. I miss the passion of doing something *right* in the world for no personal or financial gain. I firmly believe that the British Justice system is the best and fairest in the world.

CHAPTER 8
BLACK BELT

Our seven-year-old nephew, who lived six houses away from us in London, had been pushed by his parents into going to the local karate club. Every week we meet for tea and biscuits as part of the ritual of keeping in contact with the family and each time he demonstrates his martial arts ability. I play-fight with him and pretend I am a student at the Shaolin Monks' Temple in China and a trained killer. This is met with the wide eyes of innocence, which will soon be replaced by cynicism, when he realises that Father Christmas doesn't really exist. Week after week he knocks on my door on the way to his class because I have promised to come along *one day* and show them what a real karate expert is able to do.

I eventually succumb to the nagging youth and besides, I could do with a new hobby. With a little cajoling from Helen, I put on jogging pants and a baggy t-shirt and walk with him to the club. Slightly embarrassed that my nephew introduces me to the Instructor as a Shaolin Monk Disciple, I am soon leaping and jumping around with not only children, but also some of the parents, as a few have decided that they too can take up the art. Not only is this an outlet for frustration, but I have also found a form of exercise that has goals, which I never found working out at a gym.

I have never really been a great fan of sport, but karate seemed to push the right buttons in me and after many years I advance to Brown Belt. Getting there was hard and the next step to Black is only achieved by those who complete the many years of training. They reach this level when karate becomes an automatic reaction, when the fear and shock of being punched has passed, when there are no more *rabbit in the headlights* moments every time a crunching blow lands.

It is a whole year before the grading takes place and I train harder than ever to fine-tune my fighting skills. As the months pass, I become quicker and lighter. I punch much faster and harder and I now realise that the most dangerous people to fight in the Dojo are Brown Belts in training for Black; we are the ones with everything to gain on a training schedule designed for us to peak just at the right moment.

It is only by invitation from the instructor that one can attempt the Black Belt and I am delighted that I have been selected. Having reached the appropriate level after many years I am now on the run-up to the gruelling five days of the Black Belt grading. Each week, at the end of a tough, two hour training session, part of the schedule is to line-up against one's colleagues. Being in my late thirties is no excuse for not fighting younger, bigger people and the line is increased each week, from one to ten people. I sometimes wonder if a defendant in my courtroom on assault charges is aware that the Justice before them has probably had more (legal) fights in one weekend than they have had in a lifetime!

Towering over me is *Big Chris* - my next opponent - a

Black Belt who is young, flexible and at 6ft.9in. almost a foot taller than me. His speed and power is enough to knock anybody out cold, but the whole idea of karate is the ability to fight all-comers. Each week for three months I fight Chris and only on the very odd occasion do I get the upper hand. All this does is irritate him and bump him up a gear, to a level that demonstrates why he is one of the best fighters the club has ever produced.

Grading week means eight hours' training every day with the Chief Instructor, a former world champion and master in many styles of martial arts. I spend the time honing my skills for the line-up and perfecting the preset movements called *katas*. By now I find it easy to do press-ups on my front two knuckles, even on the hard stone floors. The idea is that it strengthens the wrists and means that they don't break when punching at full power.

Light sparring takes place the day before grading with fellow brown belts. Normally this means punching at half power, but on occasion this gets forgotten when the adrenaline is pumping and the opponent is on a second or third attempt to earn the elusive 'Black'.

My sparring partner is a man fifteen years younger than me and built for fighting. He is known for his aggression and is often pulled aside by the Instructors and told to calm down. We start moving around each other with jabs thrown and swirling kicks blocked by counter-strikes. His strikes are hard, his eyes focussed. I step sideways looking to place a light foot strike, when round comes his leg with the power reserved for a knockout. Crunch! Snap! His foot drives up into my ribs and an excruciating pain burns through my chest. I shout out in agony and it is obvious I have been injured. This is the green light for my opponent who continues to attack the same area. In comes his leg again, I guard my rib cage with my hands but the leg comes with such force that my fingers crack loudly. I drop to my knees with my hand in the air to stop the fight. The instructor pulls my opponent to the side and asks me if I am OK to continue. I have been injured before so perhaps this is just a lucky strike. I stand in pain and grimace as I agree to continue. In a split second comes a punch to my ribs; this is pain I had never felt before. I am withdrawn from the conflict by the instructor and sit nursing my side.

Spasms rip through my ribcage but I am still convinced it is something I can overcome. I have trained all year for this week and the final contest - I can't give up now.

Driving myself home, I am unable to steer the car with my left arm as the pain in my chest increases. I go directly to my doctor's surgery, still in my karate kit. He confirms that I have a broken rib and finger. With the pain from my rib, I hadn't even noticed the break in my finger until the doctor pointed out the deformed digit.

It will take six weeks for the rib to mend, so no grading for me. Cushioning myself in pillows, many nights are spent trying to find a good seated position as lying straight on my back pulls at the muscles and ribs, causing such pain that I can't lift myself from the bed. The spasms build in the rib area and twitch so violently that after just a few seconds my face contorts in pain and I develop dark rings around my eyes due to the sleepless nights. I question why I am doing such a tough sport. Perhaps golf would have been a better choice. But I have come so far and I am determined that I will see it through to the very end – even if it kills me. That is, if Big Chris doesn't get there first!

I have to wait a complete year before I can retake the grading. I follow the same training schedule but this time I am fitter, quicker and hungrier than before. The grading week passes without injury and the final day arrives. All I need to do is complete the ten man line up of Black Belts from 1st to 3rd Dan. Each fight lasts two minutes and the rules are simple:

1) Only use karate.
2) Do not knock out your opponent.
3) You must not be knocked out.

The first three fights pass without incident and I am exhausted. Each successive fighter is tougher and more experienced. By fight seven I'm barely able to recognise my surroundings, but the training has prepared me well and I continue to fight in an automatic karate mode. This is the sign that I have now reached the right level of expertise.

The last three fights are the longest six minutes of my life. I feel like they will never end. I am kicked so hard in the knee that I am amazed it has not broken; my movements are now slow and limited. A video playback several days later confirms that at this stage, I am now no more than a punch bag and it is clear that I am just trying to survive to the end. However, I defended well and even managed a few attacks in the final moments, something that demonstrated my karate discipline and my unbeaten fighting spirit.

On returning home, Helen, who I didn't allow to come and watch, is shocked at the bruising on my body. She tells me I look as if I have been in a car crash! The swelling and bruising increases over the coming hours and all I can do is half sit, half stand and groan in pain. No matter, I have survived and escaped with my face still recognisable as me. I know that I have done the very best I can, I blocked well and absorbed the body blows better, although this is hard to believe looking at the state of my bruised and battered body!

Several anxious weeks passed before hearing confirmation from my proud instructor that I had been awarded my Black Belt. This still remains one of *the* greatest achievements of my life.

At forty years old, following eight years of tough training, I had become a Karate 1st Dan, a skill that is recognised the world over and something that would be tested one day.

CHAPTER 9
SQUARE PEG, ROUND HOLE

Maybe it was reaching the milestone of my 40th that made me start analysing the world around me and observing the lives of other people, wondering whether they were truly happy with their lot. I often asked myself *"Do other people want more from life, like me? Perhaps I expect too much and should be satisfied with what I have."* I reflected on the past and how, even as a boy, I always wanted something more, hoping that I would find it somewhere in the future. But because life can be short, I was very aware that only a fool neglects the present.

With this in mind I took stock of all that I had – I started by looking at my surroundings..........

London is a vibrant city and we live thirty minutes on the District Line tube from Sloane Square. Our house is an old Victorian cottage, only a stone's throw from the station and in the quaint village of Kew, an idyllic spot, much sought after by many Londoners. With the Royal Botanic Gardens down the road, a popular tourist destination attracting some ten thousand people every week, one can walk the short distance from the station, through the parade of independent little shops and continue past the grand Victorian houses, now owned by people in the City or successful television personalities. Schools in the area feature highly on *The Sunday Times* best schools list and this ensures that house prices continue to rise.

The tea shop at the end of the parade is covered in beautiful flowering, hanging baskets and the proprietor has resisted the temptation to change its 1930s, old-world charm. Although his surname, Mr. Greenhouse, meant he was born to run the Kew Gardens cafe, he is a solemn bloodhound of a man, printing money from shop-made cakes and scones. His profit is increased by only employing Polish workers, who pass their jobs from one friend or relative to another, but only after they have learned enough English to get themselves more financially rewarding work – however they never master the tricky *"clotted"* cream!

Many customers are young women who have been successfully employed in the City, then landed a banker on the rise and are now the yummy-mummies of the area, marching or more likely jogging the multiple carrying pushchairs around the village to maintain a degree of fitness and sexual appeal for their husbands. Always aware of the next generation of corporate debutantes on the City conveyor belt, they are mindful that their husbands will soon be earning enough money to trade them in for a newer model, if so desired.

Chat is excitable with discussion focussed on holidays and smart restaurants. Schooling and their offsprings' brilliance will form the basis of all conversation in a few years' time, but for now the role of professional mummy has been fulfilled.

Even with all these newcomers, Kew still maintains a village atmosphere with genuine people who are decent and considerate of others. In fact, my wife describes Kew with its village green, leafy streets and sweet-natured people as the *Laura Ashley* of London, whereas trendy Highgate, its counterpart north of the river, is far more *Terence Conran*.

For several years, work has disengaged us from the daily routine of the village. I am ashamed that I cannot find the time to chat to the lovely old pensioner walking her dog around in a pushchair; this is not because she is a crazy old bird, but because the dog, once a frolicking puppy, is now the old lady in the relationship and neither can bear to be apart. The white Westie is unable to keep pace with her owner who briskly marches the four miles to her allotment everyday, where she grows her own vegetables. Like the blind man and his dog, I observe how strong and loving this bond between man and dog can become, especially when society turns its back on people who have no value or connection to their own peer group.

Friends are starting to become thin on the ground for us, as couples who vowed never to change once children entered their lives, soon realise that weekends will quickly vanish in a round of kiddies' parties and so snatched moments together as husband and wife, are precious. For them, late nights are a thing of the past, and energy levels are depleted as being a parent is a difficult task. The grandparents are using their free time to travel and enjoy the fruits of their labour, so are unavailable as a free babysitting service, available at the drop of a hat. This had been *factored-in* by the new parents, unaware that this has already been *factored-out* by the grandparents.

Being a couple who chose not to have children, the division in social conversation was turning into a chasm. Like the people who fish or play golf, and have elaborate stories of near misses, when one holds no interest in such activity then conversations become a bit stale and boring. We tried to break out of the family-centred lifestyle and search (with little success) for clubs or other social activities for people who, like us, have decided to be childfree. A search on Google returns clubs for every sexual preference or minority interest but nothing for childfree couples! If we had happened to have an interest in swinging we could have joined several clubs. The gay scene is really active, and even the alcoholics and drug addicts have social events for other like-minded folk. After another cancelled Saturday night due to a friend's babysitter not turning up, it crosses our minds that perhaps we should swap clothes, get drunk, and hang out under the railway arches with a couple of syringes!

A fellow local dog walker, whom we pass on the Kew tow path regularly, mentions that she has heard of a dog walking group that meets of an evening at various places around Richmond. We think it would be great to pursue as we could make some new friends and at the very least the dog would get some exercise. One late summer's evening we decide to bite the bullet and attend a venue, as advised, at Ham House in Richmond. We soon realise that something is odd as we approach a circle of people in the half light and notice none of them have dogs. Two men in the circle turn and look excitedly at Helen.

"It's not a dog walking group. It's a bloody dogging site!" I say to Helen as we turn on our heels and head back to the car, all the time dragging our Westie who wants to investigate the strange goings-on amongst the group.

Searching the internet, we eventually find a childfree organisation - but it is in Canada. Several emails to the founder confirm that the club does not exist outside of North America. We take the plunge and start up the London branch, soon receiving emails from other like-minded couples. Drinks and restaurant venues are arranged and several people turn up for the first meeting. Perhaps we have finally found our social outlet? Many of the people who come along are very nice, but some would turn out to be a little odd – two guys arrive thinking it was just code for - you've guessed it - swinging! This is soon rectified and they leave with tails between legs.

Once the London chapter takes hold, requests for interviews about the club come thick and fast from television and newspapers. If we are to expand beyond our local area, we need to spread the word. The Press, however, is difficult to control and much ribbing is taken from work colleagues who have witnessed us on BBC breakfast television bestowing the joys of childfree adult life. The editing team unfortunately turns what was a five hour filming session into five minutes of sound bites which portray us as wine-swilling, smug loafers with little more to do than sit around reading magazines and playing ball with our dog.

The newspapers soon latch on to our story and not a week passes without another version of how we live a childfree life. Initially-friendly journalists contact me and my comments appear in newspapers, edited and cut to such an extent that our discussion is unrecognisable. After several interviews for national papers, I learn that I am nothing more than a quick story and an easy target for derisory comments, so I reject any further requests for interviews.

Our story is later picked up by national radio which proves to be a much better vehicle for explaining our interest in starting a new social club (without the editing scissors). Many parents phone in to the live shows offering us support, some even admitting that social pressures had pushed them into having children.

A call from BBC Radio Wales invites me to Broadcasting House in London and on arrival I am rushed to a sound booth. I am to be part of a round-table discussion, but neither the presenter nor other participants are in London; they are all sitting in sound booths in other parts of the country. The only direction I receive is: *'Put these on (headphones) and wait for the red 'on air' light to come on. The producer will talk to you when the show is about to start.'*

The booth is no larger than a prison van cell, with a desk, a large clock and a massive *'on air'* sign. Ten seconds before the show starts the producer speaks into my headphones.

"You ready?"

"Yes" comes my nervous and high-pitched response.

The clock ticks and at the allotted hour the *'on air'* beacon lights up like a prostitute's sign and turns my booth into a photographer's dark room. The show starts and as I am introduced, the sweat starts to form on my brow. Within seconds I regain confidence and the one hour show passes with my little quips and comments that make the people 'round the table' laugh. At the end of the show, the producer thanks me and I am left in silence, looking at the now switched-off sign turning my room from red to grey.

I wait for what seems like an age and then realise I am expected to just get up and leave. Nobody notices as I pass the editing desks with people busy on computers and talking into headsets. Listening to the show on a podcast I think I sound relaxed and confident. I might even use this to launch a new career in radio, or maybe just let it pass and put it down to experience and fun.

Now I've been on one radio programme, I get calls from other producers who would like to fill their live shows. Often I'm working and have to make excuses to colleagues about attending a meeting offsite to make myself available for a live telephone interview. One such occasion is overtaken by terrorist threats in London and whilst doing a live interview via my mobile phone in a London square, the sound of a Chinook military helicopter overhead soon turns the broadcast on being childfree into me giving an on-the-spot news report for the station. Lots of shouting is needed in order to be heard, which only adds to the excitement of the broadcast.

"What can you see? What's happening right now?" the presenter is shouting.

"I see a large helicopter 200 feet above my head; soldiers are leaning out of the door with guns and appear to be searching the streets!"

"Is there panic on the street?"

"The helicopter appears to have seen something, they are moving closer to a section by the Euston Underpass!"

The presenter tells her listeners about the report coming in. People like to hear disaster *live*; it makes them feel part of the action. A small amount of exaggeration adds to my new career as a reporter. I assume the role with gusto and my report could have been sent from a Vietnam conflict. Every detail of the noise, the vision and the miscounted soldiers: *'I see six, no seven, no eight soldiers,'* adds to making a mundane day more exciting – maybe I should have worn a flak-jacket instead of my M&S pinstripe!

After a while, we have to accept that running this new childfree social group is not going to produce a stream of friends with similar goals in life. The only similarity is our desire not to have children and the common ground stops there - abruptly. We find some of the members to be quite anti-children, unlike us. We are caring, loving people with many nieces and nephews. In fact I am a godfather more times than *Don Corleone*! It is not that *we* are anti-children; it is just that we decided not to go down that particular path. I completely understand the fulfilment of becoming a parent and that, for some people, this gives them the greatest joy they have ever known. I cannot help how I feel and cannot explain why I have never had that yearning. My wife feels exactly the same and sometimes wishes she could share that strong mothering instinct as life would have been less isolating for her as a woman. She always says that if she had been given two lives, in one she would have had kids, but as this cannot be, she chose to be free and *for her,* motherhood always seemed to come with too many chains.

Proximity with your neighbours often forms the basis for friendship, but with most of ours either working or retired, there was a lack of people in their late thirties and early forties available during the week. My work as a contractor meant periods of unemployment, so I had time on my hands. Encouraged by my mischievous, elderly neighbour

Derek, I join a local badminton club frequented by the over sixty-fives. The venue is the local village hall which is cold from years of neglect and from useless, over-painted radiators. My initial multi-layers of clothing that I presumed would be necessary to keep me warm when playing these geriatrics, are soon discarded as the more experienced players thoroughly kick my arse. *"You will have to age a couple of decades before you're good enough for this lot!"* jokes Derek.

Living in a small cul-de-sac made up of fourteen cottages, we often see our neighbours as they hurry by on their way to work, with little more than a hello, which at weekends when time is less limited, can lead to longer conversations. Two of our dearest friends owned one of the cottages and like us, still do, but also like us, they have moved to the Riviera to become near neighbours once again.

London people are reluctant to engage and unlikely to invite people other than immediate neighbours, into their homes. We decide we need to shake the street up a little and arrange a *progressive dinner party* for all the cottages. This involves each house hosting one element of a dinner party, from drinks, starters, mains, cheese, dessert, coffee and digestifs. Timing is crucial and somebody must take on the serious job of keeping us all moving. Guess who gets lumbered with that one?

With wine glasses charged, every half an hour I herd my neighbours from one house to the next. It resembles an estate agent's day out with us all *nosying* around what is, in essence, the same basic structure - but all are decorated and amended to each occupant's taste. This annual event is much anticipated and heralded by a hive of activity, the sound of lawn mowers mowing, hedges being clipped and hoovers humming. It has bonded the occupants and created feelings of neighbourliness. As the wine flows the normally-staid librarian, No. 9, giggles uncontrollably at Derek's *nudge nudge, wink wink* comment on the size of No. 4's extension!

The little lane is exceptional in its Victorian prettiness, so much so that the council places a preservation order on the row of cottages to ensure the quaintness is retained. We knew that we were lucky to live in one of the loveliest parts of London, yet we are still unsettled.

Sunday nights are taken up with salsa dancing lessons. Our teacher is a former bank manager who wanted more from life than the bank and having won the UK championships, decided to become a full-time instructor. The ladies of the class are polite as they are pushed and pulled in every direction by we men, but when in the arms of the professional they move in a manner never before witnessed by their male partners. On occasions, the teacher's wife would attend the class and to dance with her was a joy. She probably came along to motivate the men, as one would only need to think of the next step and this would set her spinning in motion. As one friend said:

"Dancing with her is like driving a very fast car, all very exciting but one is never quite sure what will happen when you apply the accelerator."

It is a social outlet that rounds off the weekend and culminates in us all gathering in the pub afterwards for a few drinks and a chat. It is a stimulating little group that revels in a newly found exercise and from this we discover the underground world of salsa clubs, popping up all over London. As a group we decide to have a go and find ourselves in a sweaty, dimly-lit lair full of swarthy, cool dancers salsa-ing in the raunchiest manner we have ever seen.

With our bright-white smiles and polite apologies we stumble into the dancers' paths and stand out *uncoolly* as the "Kew Crew". However, as we dive into the mêlée we lose our inhibitions and are accepted into the group as the enjoyment of the dance weaves us all together.

Much as it was fun and despite two years of lessons, I never manage to progress much beyond the one, two, three, forward and backward steps. My wife on the other hand wriggles and moves like a pole-dancer, but as a partnership we are never compatible as we continually bicker about me stepping on her feet.

As the years pass and despite trying every avenue of cultural, social and professional activity, we become more unsettled with our day-to-day life. We do not have the same goals or aspirations as our friends and are unable to pinpoint any one element that *we* can change and help bring *us* back into focus with the world.

Something was missing, something was wrong, and we felt unhappy that life was never going to be any different. From the outside it appeared that we had it all: good health, happy marriage, friends and financial security. But from the inside we lacked contentment, something money cannot buy. Maybe we should have had children - would that have given us purpose to our lives? I can hear the parent reader shouting back *"Yes!"* But surely there must be other paths to tread?

CHAPTER 10
LE MANOIR

After yet another miserable wet winter in the UK, huddled against the cold in our little cottage in Kew, we decided to try a new adventure and this time we go way outside our comfort zone in both size and cost. We thought we would try buying a property abroad, somewhere sunnier, and France was our preferred option. We love France: the beautiful language, wonderful scenery, fantastic food and wine – just one problem, it's full of bloody French! Never mind, as Helen is fluent perhaps she can charm the natives.

We searched in the region of Cognac as many articles in various magazines said it was the second Côte d'Azur, but the difference was that property prices were much cheaper. After several exploratory trips to the area and viewing several charming houses, nothing particularly appealed or had that *wow* factor. Whilst thumbing through an estate agent's file, he passed quickly over a house with the words:

"You don't want zat one, it eez too big and needs lots of work."

"Oooh. Let's have a look," says Helen.

He shows us a grainy photo of a house overgrown with greenery and looking sorry with neglect, but it could not disguise the sleeping beauty underneath. As we drive up to the property, we pass through tall, imposing iron gates and sweep down a gravelly drive overrun with weeds. We pull up in front of a magnificent former cognac chateau. The house has the same elegant simplicity of Georgian architecture with its carved white stone facade and many tall symmetrical widows. Originally, this was a cognac *maison de maitre*, literally the master's house, where the owner of the vineyard lived. The house faces into an enormous courtyard encircled by old stone storage barns, the size of cathedrals. The surrounding grounds drift down towards a gigantic lake bordered by vineyards and sunflower meadows.

Excitably we push open the creaking front door and find ourselves in a cavernous entrance hall. The marble and slate floor leads to a sweeping staircase and onwards into vast, cobweb-covered rooms, each with 18th Century carved marble fireplaces. We think we have found Miss Havisham's lair. We say nothing as the agent complains about the work needed on the house, unaware of our silent enthusiasm.

We look at each other and telepathically agree that this is to be our new adventure. We had often speculated on what it would be like to own a boutique hotel, perhaps this was the opportunity to try? Obviously, with the works that needed doing, this was beyond our original budget. Even though this would involve major expenditure, our intention was to run it as a luxury boutique bed and breakfast during the summer months. We could afford to do it provided we continued working and earning a healthy income the rest of the time in London.

A few months later, the enormous *manoir* is ours. As the

property has been derelict since the war, we pull together a team of local tradesmen and import our Yorkshire builder, Mark to project manage the works. He lives on site for the entire process with regular visits from us. Mark quickly learns *builder's French* and skilfully manages the team, each week handing out the pay packets. He is helped by our lovable guardian, Monsieur Egretaud, or Eggy as we affectionately call him, who takes fatherly care of both Mark and the house. We visit and stay at the *manoir* for several weeks during the project as Helen redesigns the entire house and is on site to ensure all her specifications are included. I often hang around like a spare part as I speak not a word of French and as such cannot discuss in detail with the local artisans, the work needed.

I offer my assistance for any basic labouring jobs and so the workmen start to view me as the bottom of the food chain. I try to become part of the team and early each morning the local *boulanger* visits in his van, packed with croissants and pastries for the workers. All of us gather at the back of the parked van and enjoy the fresh buttery delights and it is not unusual for somebody to bring along a sample of their latest moonshine cognac. With a wink and a nod, we all disappear to the back of the barns and cut-off plastic bottles are passed around and filled with a rancid brew. Their grubby hands tear off pieces of baguette which we then dunk in to the gritty mixture and I enthusiastically join in with the slurping and sucking of the bread. It is utterly disgusting but I have to act like one of the lads. Suddenly we hear Helen's voice calling my name.

"C'est Madame!" comes the warning shout from one of the workmen.

With this announcement, they all scurry off in different directions and I am left holding my plastic cut-off bottle, full of booze in one hand and a soggy baguette in the other.

"What the hell are you doing?" Helen asks incredulously whilst surveying the scene.

"I am just having a drink and a bit of bread with the chaps" I say as I stand there in complete isolation.

"But it is 8:30 in the morning for God's sake! What are you doing drinking cognac at this hour? You are not setting a very good example to the team," she says in a disapproving tone. I don't even try to explain and shuffle off to my next shitty task.

Each morning, different workmen approach me holding some form of a gift for my wife, from home grown vegetables to bottles of wine. I graciously hold out my hands to accept the latest gift but they snatch it away from my grasp, guarding their treasure and indignantly exclaiming:

"Non, non. C'est pour Madame."

After seven intense months of hard work from twenty-six artisans, we transformed a once-dilapidated country house into an elegant retreat, worthy enough to be featured in several magazines. It was a good way to try life in France without breaking the umbilical cord of our lives in London and it also tapped into another dream of running a *bijou* hotel. This dream was short-lived, as after just three weeks of opening I realised that I was more Basil Fawlty than Rocco Forte. Being at the beck and call of guests was not my vocation after all. Having kicked off the first week by offering freshly squeezed juice and baked croissants with homemade jam, served at whatever hour the guests decided to rise from their beds; I quickly tired of pandering to their every whim. Breakfast was quickly replaced with concentrated juice, frozen pastries and instant coffee, only served at the allotted hour. If the guest decided to oversleep, food was removed, dumped in the bin and the table cleared. We spent the rest of the morning hiding in our wing of the house, until the time of the guest's departure, when I would appear, smile, hand over the invoice and gently push them out of the door.

During our time in the Charente, our country neighbours often invited us to dinner in an effort to welcome us to the area. Afterwards, they would gossip with friends and family about the exotic English woman and her idiot husband who could do little more than smile and laugh, only when directed to do so by his wife. Food was always some vital animal organ stuffed with the innards of another and then boiled to death. Word had obviously spread amongst the locals that I adored the dessert *Ile flottante* so this was served to me at every occasion. This was as a result of one comment made by my wife, that I loved the watery custard with whipped, poached, egg white. In fact it was her way of ensuring that I had something semi-palatable to eat. On several occasions, I would ask her what meat was being served, as it was reminiscent of an item from a Darwin's laboratory glass jar – her response was always quick and always the same

"It's a type of sausage – just eat it."

Winters were bleak amidst the dormant Cognac vineyards and the decision to part with the vast *manoir* was made easier following a heating bill of a thousand Euros for a week's worth of oil along with the various staff costs associated with maintaining such a large property.

We marketed the house for sale and eventually sold to a wealthy Scottish restaurateur for a healthy profit. However, our love affair with France continues and we immediately start looking for property in the sunnier, cosmopolitan South of France – where I will never have to eat *Ile flottante* or *Darwin's sausages* again!

Being a Londoner, the French countryside is an alien place to live. My idea of country living is something that remains a dream seen only on television. There are many stories from this period of our lives but I would be unable to do them justice in this short book. We met some wonderful characters during our time in *La France profonde* and remain proud that we brought a piece of French history back to life.

It was a great adventure and even though we were never going to feel at home in the Charente, the experience was a breath of fresh air. It was in fact, a turning point for us and helped to show us the path ahead.

CHAPTER 11
THE CHANGE

Management consultant - this is a term used by companies for independent contractors who are prepared to work hard, have no job security and who are often despised by fulltime staff. The advantage is that the money can be fantastic and it does allow you to move from one company to another without the stigma of not being able to hold down a job.

Most contractors register with online recruitment search engines. The words of their *curriculum vitae* are carefully crafted to include as many corporate buzz words as possible so that when a recruitment agent runs a word search, up pops the CV, right at the top of the pile. The agent quickly dials the always-contactable mobile number - they must be quick as every other agency is working on a numbers game too and so they must get *their* consultant in front of the client first. If successful the agency gets twenty five percent of the consultant's daily rate. Everybody makes a cut, everybody wants a cut, but if the consultant fails he gets cut.

My next job as a consultant is at Tower Bridge, working for the Greater London Authority. I travel to their headquarters, a glass testicle-shaped building known locally as *the bollock*, on the banks of the Thames directly overlooking the City. My role is to engage with minority groups across London and to assist them in obtaining building contracts. This is supposed to ensure a fair spread of work across small companies who employ disabled, minority ethnics or LGBTs (Lesbians, Gays, Bi-sexuals and Transgenders). Even on my first day I already suspect that this would be harder than finding a teetotal university student, but the prospect of buying a dream holiday villa on the French Riviera keeps me motivated.

Over the following weeks, I encourage companies to tick the box if they have employees who fall into these categories. If only I could find that elusive disabled, cross-dressing, transsexual, brickie who is not sure if he/she is lesbian or gay, then I would hit the jackpot!

I enter the lift from the foyer with an armless man and it crosses my mind to ask if he is any good at building work. We wait for a few seconds and then it dawns on me that we are not going anywhere unless either I press, or he pecks, a floor button. Arriving at our level, I follow him out of the lift and on reaching my desk I am greeted with glee by my colleague whose chair backs onto mine. My chair-to-chair buddy is a gay dwarf. I politely ask about his weekend but his replies are met by my disinterested smile as I start to fidget. I am here to work, not chat and anyway, conversations conducted at my crotch level make me feel very uncomfortable.

My job is very well paid but doesn't give me a title to mark out where I am to be pigeonholed. This pushes me down the pecking order to such a level that on my way to a meeting with the Deputy Mayor, I am told by my adolescent manager that I am not to directly address the *Mayoral*

Majesty-in-waiting!

"Keep yer marf shut, yeah. Yoos is there to just take the minutes man, you know what I mean, yeah?"

I bite my tongue and think of France.

After a useless meeting we break for lunch and I leave the office looking for a sandwich bar.

"Is there anything else you would be wanting today?" a disembodied voice asks as I am passed my BLT.

"A new life?" is my retort that stumps the voice into silence.

The lunchtime drizzle now starts to come down in buckets, so I shuffle towards a vacated window stool which is comfortable enough to consume my sandwich in minutes, but not comfortable enough to encourage me to spend all afternoon there. The breast pocket of my shirt is vibrating madly as my phone rings; it's Helen, who is in the South of France staying with her brother, whilst looking for a holiday home.

I answer with the vocal rhythm reserved for one's spouse; not the excited voice first used in the early part of the relationship, more of a flat tone reflecting my mood. She is sitting in the sunshine at the local tennis club with her brother Phil and his wife Sue, enjoying a fresh salad of local produce which actually has flavour, unlike the brightly coloured and tasteless mush I am eating. She says it is sunny, the people are lovely and she is enjoying a great glass of chilled rosé.

I have little to discuss apart from the political correctness of my office. But today she is not interested and talks happily about the weather and laughs at casual comments being made in the background. Bad temperedly, I wonder why she doesn't finish her conversation *before* calling me. We talk about her day and the viewings arranged for later in the afternoon. I finish our call and my soggy sandwich, promising to call her later.

The office is never far from the lunchtime filling station and I rush through the downpour with other hurrying people, all keen to avoid overexposure to the rain, which will leave our clothes damp for the remainder of the day.

The Spotty Boss calls me into his office to discuss my progress and the results expected during my short contract. This chat is never going to be friendly. It is obvious he thinks I am too old and did not want me in the first place - I was simply imposed on him from a great height. He has swallowed a management paperback and uses phrases learned but not understood.

"So what sort of progress, yeah, have you made on the deliverables my man? My charts ain't looking that good, yer know what I mean, yeah?" he says in his patronising tone.

"Well let's be honest, it is hardly the easiest contract to fulfil. I am not allowed to prompt people into saying they meet our criteria, yet I need to establish if they do!" I reply.

"There are ways around it, yeah, if you try harder brov, yeah."

"Have you ever tried to casually chat to some hairy-arsed builder and ascertain if he spent the weekend dressing in his wife's knickers? You are likely to get your face punched in," I reply, doubting that such a situation is documented in his manual.

Whilst discussing what is expected from my contract I hear a voice in my head repeating my horoscope from today's *Daily Mail*, '*monotony is the only reward of the cautious*'. I maintain a degree of decorum whilst I listen to The Spotty Boss spouting off and using irritating terminology popular amongst his peer group. I can take no more.

"Listen." I interrupt. *"I am not your brother. Nor am I your man. And finally, please stop using the expression "yeah" and "you know what I mean" in every sentence, because I don't know what you mean. O.K?"*

He sits in silence.

"Let's be honest, this is a crap job, the deliverables are unrealistic and I don't know what I am doing here? In fact why am I here? In fact I don't even want to be here! In fact I quit!

No further conversation is needed looking at the reaction on his bewildered face.

I stand up and say *"Listen man, good luck in your career, yeah, brover, you know what I mean, yeah?"* I suck my teeth and wink as I depart the room.

The feeling of liberation is immense as I walk out of the building. Having thrown caution to the wind, the heavy weight of years of meaningless, monotonous toil has been lifted off my shoulders - maybe the fortune teller in the *Daily Mail* was right after all.

The rain stops and the streets are clear apart from a few tourists laughing casually and enjoying the picturesque views of the City. Suddenly I have a spring in my step. I'm heading for the tube station for what I hope is my last working day in London.

The train carriage is clear of people. Those onboard have seats and vacant ones stare at me like prizes, inviting me to choose whichever one I want. I stretch my legs out indulgently, not having to worry about rush-hour boots and sharp stiletto heels. Heading back to the sanctuary of home, *this* is the day when my life is going to change. I am going to do something before monotony imprisons me with a life sentence.

Sitting in my favourite armchair with thoughts rushing, I am jolted by the ring of the phone. Helen is surprised to hear me in such a buoyant mood.

"How did you get on with the viewings?" I ask.

"Fantastic! I think I have found a place for us, you will love it! Anyway how was your day?"

"Fantastic! I quit my job!"

Silence fills the air.

"Well that's it then" she says emphatically as I wait to be chastised, *"Nothing to stop us now – let's take the leap and go!"*

Unlike many wives who would have despaired at the loss of my large income, she is delighted that I have left the ever-turning wheel and we decide to make plans for a new venture. We have some investments, but not nearly enough to call ourselves retired, yet the sum is sufficient to be our springboard into the new horizon.

Much planning takes place and redecoration of our Kew

house, to enable us to rent out the property and provide additional income. Our new tenants fall in love with our pretty cottage and adore the local village. Packing and clearing quickly follows with plenty of trips to the local refuse dump to free us of knick-knacks acquired over the years, trophies of money burnt. We give away as much as possible and leave a house furnished to a level that makes it feel homely.

Free at last. South of France here we come.......

CHAPTER 12
AU REVOIR ENGLAND

I have quit my job.

My wife has folded her business.

We have rented out our cottage.

Cars have been sold - except the one to get us to France.

Goodbyes have been said.

Money is in the bank.

The car is packed.

The dog is loaded.

The dog is squawking.

The dog is jumping around the car.

Au Revoir Angleterre!

CHAPTER 13
BRICKS AND MORTAR

When living in London, the dream of owning a house in the South of France is more than buying a property - it is about buying into endless summers, drinking wine on a terrace whilst watching the sun setting over the mountains. The reality is often ugly, overpriced houses presented by agents who will charge an extortionate six per cent for very little work. Often the property has been poorly built and even more poorly maintained - especially if it belongs to one of the many second-home owners who have tired of providing a *free holiday* for friends and family. We had already experienced the *Grand Tour* by our English friends at the *manoir* and were not prepared for the second invasion once we found our property on the Riviera. This time we were buying a house for *us,* not for an extended circle of *friends* who wanted to be suddenly *reunited.*

When searching for a new home in England, one is used to seeing houses of character which are solidly constructed, built during the Victorian and Edwardian period. Having owned two lovely Victorian cottages in London and a beautiful Georgian apartment in Bath, we were no strangers to the process of renovating old properties. However, in the South of France even the new houses can be poorly constructed and thrown up at minimal cost. My wife and I often refer to these properties as *architects' vomit*! A prominent estate agent in the area, who is now a friend, confirmed my suspicions by saying that the property market is *ninety per cent shit* and *ten per cent overpriced!* Agents rarely take into account the location, aspect and character of a property when valuations are made, instead using a blunt square meter calculation for both building and land.

We search intensively for a character property and we always apply the same testing question to every property we see:-

'Does the house feel like it is on the Côte d'Azur?'

Many of the properties we looked at were perfectly adequate, but we wanted something special. We had no problem with a renovation project but some houses were little more than a pile of stones. Some had potential with lovely views, but unless you had a couple of mules and a team of Sherpas you would never get up the driveway. We wanted something special with a touch of magic.

After looking at over fifty properties, we eventually unearthed a little gem. It was a pretty part-stone villa with a turret looking out over the hills of the Esterel and down to the coastline of Theoule-sur-mer. It was at the end of a cul-de-sac and next to a small wood which the agent highlighted as a selling point, enthusing about its privacy and security.

We bought it from an elderly couple who used the house as a second home. On the surface it looked like a simple redecoration job. After one week of living there we realised that (as is so often the case in France) the sewage pipes were blocked. This was despite having the certificate from the *Mairie's* appointed agent who verified that the system was working correctly. Upon inspection, we soon discovered a grease-blocked kitchen waste-pipe and a sewage pipe which had healthy tree roots almost appearing in the toilet bowl!

After less than a year, we finished the renovation of the house and garden, cutting back trees to reveal stunning views across the valley. The downside of opening up the garden was that petty thieves and burglars could now observe us from the little wood and several break-in attempts were made. Added to this, we were confronted with a new problem.

A bank statement lands on the door mat. We look in horror at the dwindling balance and Helen turns to me and says:

"There is nothing else for it. You know what we should do now?"

I suddenly have visions of me sitting on the tube strangled by my tie and facing the drizzle and grey of London.

"I cannot go back." I plead.

"Good God no! — I don't mean that. Why don't we sell and buy another?"

We market the property for sale and within a few weeks receive a full asking price offer.

Back on the hunt again, we find a charming 1920's villa with staggering views across the whole of the bay of Cannes and the countryside of the hinterland. It has only two bedrooms at the moment but with Helen's skills we know that we can rearrange the space to create a four bedroom villa - simple compared to the monumental task of the one thousand square meter *manoir!*

Our friends and neighbours used Polish builders to renovate their house from top to bottom. They could not recommend them highly enough, so we decide not to succumb once again to the local French artisans who have a clear cut-off point for work. An electrician will make the hole for his cables but it is not his job to fill the hole, instead you have to have a plasterer who will fill that hole, but he will not sand and paint the hole, that is the job of the decorator. The problem is that estimates seem reasonable, but the mistake most people make, as we did, is to assume that a quote is for the complete job, whereas it is not. All other trades have to be factored in, which then adds up to an expensive piece of work. The Polish on the other hand will do the whole job and always try to finish to northern European specifications – they do not always succeed however!

Work begins for an agreed daily amount as we figure it is better to have them on-site and working on minor tasks while Helen redesigns the house. Afterwards when she has drawn up the plans we will get a fixed price for each job. However, it becomes clear after a couple of days that they are in fact illegal workers. Despite being in France for ten years, they have existed under the radar of the authorities. This means three things: more money can be sent back to the family in Poland, enough is left over for rent in a grotty part of town, and finally, crucially, there is money left for the big drinking weekends. It is clear that one of the two has a severe problem with alcohol and with the increasing heat of the summer he becomes dehydrated by midday! He is a functioning alcoholic.

We are one week into the project when the boozy builder comes running in to the house with a t-shirt clasped over his inflated stomach. Whilst using a circular saw to cut the bottom off a door, it has slipped. He was using a machine which he won playing cards, from a friend, who in turn had been given it by a friend because the safety guard was broken! A slight trip of the saw meant it flew through the air and across his stomach, then, continuing on, removed the top of his finger.

Blood is gushing from the wound and on removal of his t-shirt to explain the accident, we see it is so deep that the yellow fat layer is clearly visible. This is a major injury and needs hospitalisation, immediately.

"Drive me to the hospital and leave me. I am working illegally and you will get in trouble." He groans as shock turns his face white.

In France, employing illegal labour is not the problem of the labourer, it is the problem of the person for whom they are working. The state considers you to be exploiting the worker and will support him in every situation. As such, any fines imposed by the state are on the home owner and the labourer simply disappears from the job and appears down the road the following day on another job.

The cut is so serious that an ambulance has to be called. We decide that we will pay all medical expenses rather than having a dead Pole on our consciences. In France, the ambulance service is provided by the *pompiers* (firemen). They are well respected, trained paramedics as well as firefighters. He is strapped up by the firemen and taken off to the hospital on a stretcher. Whilst being carried to the medic van he is mumbling incoherently to my wife.

"What is it Marius?" she asks. *"Do you want me to get a message to your family? Do you have any last words?"*

With one arm in the air, he moans:

"I have left a bottle of beer in the freezer and I am afraid it will explode!"

We complete the renovations with a reputable building company and short of funds, rent the house out for two summers. We start to feel *house rich, penny poor* and decide it would be nice to fill the coffers again. Vastly differing valuations from agents mean we set the price that we believe is correct. There is a flurry of interest and then suddenly the housing market collapses. All buyers seem to disappear off the face of the earth. We ride the scary financial roller-coaster once again and after reducing the house price we find a buyer in the spring. The couple are looking to retire at some point and after many years of searching, decide to buy our charming and unique house, earlier than they had intended. We make a healthy profit, they find the house of their dreams - everybody is happy.

Here we are once more; the local agents are now familiar friends and know we are looking for another needle in a hay-stack. Much searching takes place before the completion of our sale, but every property has issues with structure or location. One agent drives us the short distance from her office claiming she has just the right place for us. As we come over the brow of the hill, we see breathtaking views down to Nice and the Cap d'Antibes and she points out a red house in the middle of an olive grove. Our hearts pound, *"this could be the one"*, we both think, even before we have arrived. The house was constructed seven years earlier and is owned by a gay couple who are divorcing. Due to a dispute with the builder, it has not been completed internally. Every room is painted a garish colour and there are no internal walls, even between bedrooms and bathrooms. The kitchen is in the garage, and there is inadequate drainage and just as we near completion we become aware that the house has no legal conformity (official approval that the house exists and has been constructed as per the original agreed plans).

We head to the mayor's office with our *notaire* and after much discussion confirm that if we complete the work, move the kitchen and install a now-obligatory rain-soak-away-tank, called a *bassin*, we will get conformity and make our house legal and thus more valuable.

We eventually move in six months after selling our house. Despite having all the usual certificates that the place functions properly, (and in the hope that a newly constructed house would in fact have working toilets), I realise that Christmas Day will be spent up to my elbows in shit once again! Months pass and renovations are almost complete and the obligatory swimming pool is installed. Despite the house being fantastic, it does not stop our longing to have something on the coast one day.

We will renovate several more properties before cashing in and buying our luxury beach hut! Until such time we will keep moving and enjoy the time we spend together.

Me. My wife. And the dog.

CHAPTER 14
COPS AND ROBBERS

Although people expect a certain level of criminality on the French Riviera, it is not exclusive to just that part of the country. At the start of our journey to a new life, little did we know that we were to get the full Gallic tour of crime!

Setting off, we load what looks like the entire contents of our London house into the back of our people-carrier. We decide to drive as far as possible before stopping for an extended break, so that we will be sufficiently charged for another eight-hour drive. This takes us to just outside the suburbs of Paris, where we find a motorway service station with restaurants, shops and a motel. Not wanting to draw attention to our overloaded car, we park it within view, but also away from the main throng. When we return, we notice that one of the tyres is flat. Unable to retrieve the spare from the floor under all the luggage, Helen goes to the public phone kiosk to find a number for a local garage, as all the insurance documents with emergency numbers are buried somewhere in the back of a vehicle which now resembles a Pickford's removals van.

A simple call to a local breakdown service would help us on our way, but while looking through the Yellow Pages her handbag is snatched by a man who jumps onto a scooter with his accomplice and then accelerates off at speed. Her money, bank cards and phone have disappeared in a second and Helen is left shocked and annoyed.

Eventually she gets a number and a breakdown truck arrives and takes us to the repair centre just five minutes away. It becomes clear from talking to the mechanic that his garage is kept busy with regular work provided by the actions of local thieves. He tells us that they use nail guns to fire nails into the tyres! They deliberately target people who have cars laden with luggage and they normally operate by deflating two tyres, knowing that most cars have only one spare. They hope that the drivers are unable to have the car removed and will instead spend the evening at the conveniently located hotel within the service station complex. Later that night, the thieves will return and empty the contents of the car at leisure.

Over the next few months, Helen's credit card is used at the same *péage* (toll), on the same stretch of motorway, at approximately the same time every day. Reporting this to the police, she is astounded that the information is met with much apathy and lots of Gallic shrugs.

Crime is never spoken about on the Côte d'Azur, especially by the estate agents who are selling a dream of endless sunshine and a lifestyle associated with the rich and famous. Only after a while do you start to understand some of the problems in the region. The area can be broken down as follows: Nice being a vibrant, urban centre has many no-go areas, whereas Cannes is a smaller chic resort where policing is more visible. In the back country, further away from the coast, some villages are heavily populated by the English, Dutch and Scandinavians who are viewed by thieves, often incorrectly, as wealthy targets.

In the summer months, crime shifts to the holiday hotspots and one can easily recognise a potential target. Foreign-plated cars driven by carefree tourists cruise the coast roads, unaware as they dangle their Rolex-wristed bait from the car window, that they are giving off a scent to the circling sharks. After stalking their prey, the thieves strike at the first opportunity. It is easy to see why those who have lots of money decamp to the safe, but visually unpleasant haven of Monaco. Wherever you go in the principality, a camera will be monitoring your every move with the police standing on street corners, ready to arrest even the litterlouts!

Having recently moved to the South of France, we start to enjoy the carefree lifestyle on offer, blissfully unaware that we are about to experience our *own* nightmare of crime.

On our first New Year's Eve on the Riviera, we attend a party at a friend's house and amongst the guests was a man renowned for his wandering hands. We decide to leave early before my wife, or even I, get touched up and head home around 1am.

We drive up to our house and get out of the car and hear our neighbours still celebrating. I notice that our front gate is very slightly ajar. *I thought I had locked the gate when we left home* - I immediately suspect something as I know that I would not have been so careless. We walk the ten steps down from the gate to the front door when I hear a banging from *inside* the house. My heart races and I quietly unlock the front door. As I slowly push the door open, I see the TV hanging off the wall; the bedroom, which is on the same level, has been turned upside down and bags and clothes strewn about. I step forward and let out a mighty war cry.

The banging stops and I hear footsteps coming down the stairs from the turreted office, just off the kitchen. An athletic young man runs down the stairs and, slipping on the last step, he drops a heavy crowbar in his hurry to escape. I give chase through the kitchen, and then the bedroom, where he exits via the broken patio door on to the terrace, all the while being chased by me. He is wearing trainers which give him grip on the shiny surface. I am wearing leather-soled shoes so traction becomes difficult. He soon outpaces me and disappears quickly out of sight.

Suddenly, I hear Helen scream from the front door: *"He's here!"*

I turn and run back, picking up the crowbar as I rush to Helen. The burglar has made his way around the house and headed for the front gate which I locked on our return. Unable to escape, he runs down the steps and turns towards the bushes bordering our neighbour's garden, which has a wire fence, embedded deep in the bramble growth. He is half-way over when I get there and I launch myself at the hedge, not caring about the needles tearing into my skin. I'm not able to reach him because of the thickness of the bush, but I can see his backside clambering over the fence.

Mad with rage, I scream at the burglar *"You fucking bastard!"* as I ram the pointed end of the crowbar up his backside.

"You fucker!" I shout as I shove the crow bar up his arse for

a second time with such force that he is undoubtedly injured.

No sound comes from the escaping burglar as he pulls himself over the fence with his trailing legs twitching and contorting. We can sense his fear as he frantically tries to escape from these two elegantly dressed Brits screaming and hurling abuse at him in French and English. My years of karate training have kicked in. I am unafraid. When it came to it, I was swift in movement and thought. Having faced Big Chris, few men scare me.

A shockwave of fury hits us along with a feeling of having been abused and invaded. Once back inside the house we notice several items have disappeared which the fleeing burglar didn't have on him, so there must have been an accomplice. I notice that they have emptied the holdall containing my karate kit, obviously to be used as their swag bag. It must have caused them a moment of concern as they removed my Black Belt, swords and boxing gloves!

We realise that we don't know the emergency number for the local police, so frantically we call a friend at the party, who tells us to dial 17. The police response is cool and uninterested. It is not until my wife relays my attack on the burglar that the tone changes and within ten minutes several *Gendarmes* arrive at our house. Their attitude to the burglary itself is lukewarm but they are very interested in my assault on the intruder. After some questioning, and a mention by me that I am a magistrate, their approach changes and the now uneasy, sergeant phones the local chief of police. Less than twenty minutes later the chief is standing in our kitchen, chatting casually.

"Don't worry. I will ave my offizers call ze local ozpitals to zee if zey ave bin any recent admissions for a man wiz three arseholes!"

The police leave our house once they have arranged for my fingerprints to be taken at the station the following day. Despite the burglar's blood on the brambles, it is useless, as I'm informed, wrongly, that no DNA database exists in France. We go to bed for what seems like an endless night, the house creaks and cracks with noises never heard before and we are in such a heightened state of alert that even our heartbeats sound loud.

Prints are taken at the station and we receive a friendly, off the record word from the chief, who suggests we be a little careful, as there is a chance the burglars might return, either for revenge or simply to come back for the booty. Little did we realise just how much these words would ring true and how it would lead to many months of fear and self-inflicted imprisonment.

Barely a week passes when on our way home from an evening out, Helen senses that we are being followed. She is uneasy about a car just behind us with no lights on. I park at the end of our dark, isolated cul-de-sac but a sense of foreboding makes me edge forward and shine my headlights on *full beam* down the road. She was right! Ahead of us is a car driving very slowly, in reverse, with its boot open. Inside sit two men and outside, walking towards us, are another two, one of them carrying a large bag. We get out of the car and head towards them shouting:

"Qu'est ce que vous faites la? What are you doing there?"

They continue to walk towards us in silence. Hearing our

cries, our neighbour has come outside and shouts out that she is calling the police. Hearing her threat, they throw the bag into the open boot, jump in the car and speed off. Adrenalin pumping, we are determined to get their registration number so we rush back to our car and accelerate so fast over the bumps in the road, that we ground the underside of our BMW several times. We must have taken a wrong turn at the top of the road as there is no longer any sign of them.

Two weeks later, we are in bed when an alarm, which we think is a pool alarm, wakes us up. We hear noises but decide we are just being paranoid, so we go back to sleep. It is only when our French neighbour asks if we are OK the next morning, that we find out that there were three carloads of men outside the house trying to steal the BMW (this was the alarm we heard) and trying to get inside the property boundaries which had been secured following the first forced entry. Apparently, she wanted to call the police but her husband told her not to get involved! He decided that being British we had probably brought it on ourselves!

A fortnight passes without incident then at 2 o'clock one morning we hear the noise of somebody forcing open the shutters to our second bedroom. We sit in the dark waiting to see if we can make out how many people are trying to break in. We see an outline of two men at the bathroom window. Hastily pulling on some clothes, I then turn on the light. The noise seems to stop for a few seconds but then continues. It appears that knowing we have stirred is not going to stop them. Common sense says we should *not* leave the house as this is now turning into a vendetta provoked by the original assault. We stay inside our locked bedroom and call the police who by now have our number programmed into their system. They arrive in minutes and armed officers patrol the gardens and find an entry point. The burglars have disappeared, empty-handed once again.

A further two attempts are made, by how many we don't know. We get into the habit of driving twice around roundabouts to ensure nobody is behind us, when entering our road. Living under siege was not what we came for, so we put the house on the market, despite having only just finished the renovations and only living in it for twelve months. At a party shortly afterwards, we are advised by a friend *not* to talk about our experiences if we want to sell our house as 'word spreads like wild fire' in the close expat community. This was evident when a couple, new to the area, start to relay the story of *our* events - to us! The story is exaggerated and expanded to such an extent that we are forced to correct them and explain that they have now met the celebrity victims!

Fortunately for us the house sells within weeks and even though we keep in contact with the new owners, our scary tale has never been mentioned by either party - although we are sure that they know. They have three dogs which is always a good deterrent and thankfully they have never had a problem with 'unwanted visitors'.

Somerset Maugham famously labelled the South of France as "*a sunny place for shady people*" and it is easy to understand how some become involved in crime once they become a victim. We received little help from the police - an apathetic officer even suggested that if we were so worried about it, we should go back to our own country! In reality there was little likelihood of them ever solving the case, so one could easily turn to taking matters into one's own hands or calling on the services of some of the unsavoury characters who slink around the Riviera. Unsolicited, I am approached at a party by a wide-boy expat.

"Listen son, I heard about your recent bit of bovver. Look, I can send a few of the boys down. Trap a few fingers in car doors. That will soon sort 'em owt," he says with hands held apart as if he has just offered me a deal not to be missed.

"It is a very kind offer but...." I say before he interrupts me.

"No problem son. Don't worry about paying me. Let's just see it as a favour," as he places his hand on my shoulder. *"I am sure one day you can do something for me. Know what I mean?"*

Maybe he thinks I can be useful to him either as a black belt or as a magistrate. He has the wrong man. Fortunately I am a level-headed person who believes in the justice system, but I can see how some people could become disillusioned and turn to these vigilantes.

Sadly, crime is not rare, and one soon discovers that almost everyone who has decided to call this place their home has been affected. A few have even been gassed while in bed asleep and only discover the burglary on waking up with a massive headache, to the sight of a home turned upside down. Others have been attacked at the gates to their house and robbed of their car and jewellery. In the more affluent Cap d'Antibes, Cap d'Ail and Mougins, homeowners have even been subjected to more serious ordeals involving guns.

It is rare for weapons to be used in the suburbs; this is the training ground for the burglar and it is really only in the very wealthy areas when they need to get past security systems, guards and dogs, when guns become the weapons of choice.

Once aware of the problems down here, one learns to adapt. We have now moved to a more discreet area, further away from the crime hotspots and we now have permanent neighbours, secure fencing and an alarm and we own a couple of ordinary French cars that do not distinguish us from the masses. Having taken these simple precautions, we have not become victims again.

Remember though that crime is not unique to France – the bogeyman can get you wherever you are. If this is your bedtime read, sleep tight........

CHAPTER 15
RICHES TO RAGS

In the Riviera, there is a distinct lack of well-paid work outside of tourism, the airlines, yachting and associated industries. There is a technology park called Sophia Antipolis which used to be the Silicon Valley of France but with taxation and rising costs of employing staff, the majority of these companies have been squeezed out. What remains is mainly low level and poorly paid technical work.

We still needed to earn a living and so with this in mind, I decided to turn my hand to becoming an internet entrepreneur. I started a website, along with three previous work colleagues, around the issue of court sentencing. The website allowed the public access to a simple drop down menu of offences and the likely corresponding sentence to be passed. We intended making our money by charging solicitors to be on the site, so when a person required a lawyer, they could use the ones listed.

What we had not foreseen was the government changing the way in which Legal Aid is given, so to cut a very long story short, lawyers started to withdraw and moved across to Immigration Law where the money was re-allocated. After just a short period, we had to close down with a small loss, but not before it had been reported on by various news agencies. On the back of this minor success, I was invited by an obscure channel on SKY TV to make a short series of programmes about the law.

My brush with TV fame takes me to a warehouse in the middle of Birmingham. The channel is short of money so external filming is the cheapest option and licences asking for permission to film in certain locations is overlooked. It is more a case of *'get on with it and hope for the best.'* After several 'takes' as I keep forgetting my words, I throw away my carefully crafted script and talk about what I know, the subject of sentencing options in the magistrates' court. To toughen up the programme's image, I am asked to wear jeans and my battered black leather jacket. With my tough guy approach I am referred to by my cameraman as the Vinnie Jones of the legal profession! Not an opinion shared by the *Radio Times* critic – I am embarrassed to tell you what he thought of my TV debut.

My foray into television gives me a taste for doing more. As an interior designer and experienced lecturer, Helen has had some success as a TV presenter, showcasing home interiors products on a major shopping channel, popular with middle-aged, middle England. The production team think that I might be a male version of her. An invitation to attend the studio and discuss various options quickly follows and when my interview hour arrives I barely walk five steps into the room in my TV garb of torn jeans and battered black leather jacket, when the producer, who has watched me from the very first step, says in a loud voice:

"No! Thank you! Not for us!"

Without even breaking step, I walk in a circle and straight out of the door, before it has even had chance to close after my initial entrance!

Whatever the reason, it is my shortest interview ever. Much amusement and ribbing from Helen follows and there endeth my career in TV.

For many, like us, the best way of making money is to rent out your home to holiday-makers for the summer period. The property must be desirable and as long as you are happy to let complete strangers take over your house, the eight to ten week rental period can provide a substantial amount of money.

In order to succeed and attract quality customers, the house needs to be in excellent order and have a *wow* factor. You need a great website with lots of information and glossy photos to ensure your property stands out from the crowd. With my technical abilities, I created mine and others' websites and Helen dressed the house to magazine standard. We are very privileged to have lived in some beautiful houses amidst stunning scenery and this has attracted many wishing to share in our dream of living in the South of France - if only for a short while.

Moving out for the summer season can be like moving house as all personal and expensive items have to be rehomed too. Cheaper temporary accommodation has to be found to make it all worth doing. We have often waved goodbye to the happy holiday-makers, now settled in to our luxury villa and driven down the road to find ourselves ten minutes later sitting in a friend's chalet – posh garden shed - for two weeks. We move around all summer like gypsies, house-sitting for friends. We are much in demand as we leave the house in great order with me having fixed things and Helen having given it a mini makeover. We often holiday during this period on the beautiful Cap d'Antibes and rent a stunning little cottage close to the beach. We love the area so much that we plan to make this place our home one day once we unearth our own little gem.

As Helen is an interior designer and I am very handy with the hammer we have never been afraid to restore houses. It was never our intention to become *serial renovators* but due to circumstances beyond our control it became a logical and novel way to survive. Besides, we seem to be very good at it and we like the fact that we don't have to answer to anyone. Or so we thought!

One day, out of the blue a recorded delivery letter landed in our post-box. It had an official looking stamp and the brown envelope reserved for government organisations. It requested that we attend the office of a tax inspector the following week. We are advised by our accountant that if there is nothing to hide then we should save ourselves a considerable sum by preparing the documentation and presenting it ourselves. Taking his advice, we spend hours endlessly checking and preparing the necessary information.

What troubled us was why we had been singled out for a full tax inspection when we had always done everything completely above board. Although we had worked at developing new businesses, we hadn't actually earned a traditional income for four years. Our only income was from our long term tenants in Kew and our summer rentals in France.

Our fear of meeting the dreaded tax inspector was unfounded as he turned out to be not only a smashing chap, but also, according to my wife, quite a hunk. He was very helpful and guided us through the process. He explained that we had been flagged as potential tax evaders for two reasons. The first was because we had moved house within just one year and as we had made a very healthy profit, the French tax authorities believed that we were doing it as a commercial property venture. This extremely fast turnaround was explained away once he saw the police reports of our burglaries.

The second reason was because on the contract of sale, I had put my job title down as a magistrate, as the lawyer had insisted that I fill in the box on his form. In France, this is a highly paid profession, unlike in England where it is voluntary. They thought I was earning a vast income and not declaring it. Once we'd explained this to the tax man we asked him if he found any hidden money would he be so kind as to let us know because we could do with the cash! His wry smile made us realise that we had nothing to worry about and a few months later we received the letter confirming that our tax affairs were all in order. My wife was very disappointed that we would not be going back to see the hunky tax inspector again.

Since then we have earned some money from Helen's activities as a talented artist and she still does some interior design work for friends. I have undertaken a minor management consultancy role for a local estate agency. We also intersperse our work with renovating our home; however, we realise that we will never be in the financially enviable position once achieved in London. Phone calls from the bank offering us loans are now rare: they are quick to offer you an umbrella during the sunny days of earning money and even quicker in asking for it back when it starts to rain.

We get by on our own wits and even though we do not have as much money to fritter on gourmet dinners and gadgets, we would choose this life any day over the one we had before. We feel richer than ever.

CHAPTER 16
THE RELUCTANT GUARDIAN

If you buy a second home in another country, it is vital to have somebody to look after the place. Someone needs to be available to let workmen in, to be able to speak the language and to arrange whatever is necessary to ensure that the house is not left to rot. Known as a *guardien* in France, the closest comparison in England would be a caretaker.

When we owned the *manoir*, *Eggy* was our trusty guardian. He was in his early seventies and looked like the French cartoon character, Asterix the Gaul. He had the spirit and physical ability of a far younger man and had a twinkle in his eye that made him endearing. *Eggy* was vital to the running of the grand house and invaluable in getting the right workmen during the major renovation. He acted like a site foreman hiring and firing those whom *he* thought were not up to scratch. But at times it felt like *his* house, not ours. Even though we loved *Eggy* to bits, there were occasions when we would have liked our privacy. I remember one day when Helen decided that she wanted an all over tan and laid out on a towel on the sunny terrace.

"Ça va Helene?" Eggy said as he popped his head over the wall, *"I ave ze lovely melons for you."*

As Helen tried to cover up, he decided that he would give her an hour-long lecture on how he grew his famous Charentaise melons - all the time his eyes darting up and down admiring hers.

For foreigners living in the South of France, being a guardian is a good way to make a living. Many are very responsible people and are often available around-the-clock. Some guardians not only take care of the house but they are also able to arrange anything from dinner parties to weddings, if required.

We sold our house in the hills behind Cannes to a lovely couple who intended to use the place once they retired from a busy life in the Far East. Until then they would rent the house throughout the year to holiday-makers. They were in need of a guardian and although I knew the house inside-out I was reluctant to offer my services, as I had already started on our next renovation project. It had often occurred to me that I would make a competent guardian, but I didn't fancy it - I had enough *shit* of my own to deal with! They asked if I could recommend someone, but the people I knew were fully booked. They had no luck in finding a guardian so I eventually recommended Spencer, whom I knew on a semi-social level. He seemed a decent sort of chap, a recognisable character with his exuberant RAF moustache and his Terry Thomas breezy manner. However, I could not vouch for his professional abilities.

When we rented the house during the summer months I produced a manual detailing every item so guests could refer to this book if needed. It was the perfect guidebook for any new caretaker. I arranged to meet Spencer at the house to go through all the details of the property to ensure a smooth handover. I gave him the extensive manual so thereafter all questions could be answered by him.

Spencer is late. I have waited two hours and can now expect one of his many excuses which at times border on complete fantasy.

"Hello mate. Sorry about being late. I was caught up in a terrible traffic accident in Valbonne. Blood and guts everywhere. Anyway, I am here now so let's start," he says.

We go through every item but I can see by his glazed eyes I am fast losing his attention - another liquid lunch being the likely cause of his concentration deficit.

Heavy rain is forecast for the weekend and I show Spencer the external drain that needs to be kept clear of autumn leaves, otherwise there is danger of water flooding the house.

"Yes mate, no worries," he says in his usual buoyant tone.

Torrents of rain bucket down as is typical for November in the South of France. I receive a call from my old neighbour who has been unable to get hold of Spencer. He tells me that the water is starting to rise by the drain at our old house. I phone Spencer and tell him that he needs to sort out the problem, fast.

"No problem mate. I will pop up there later."

Why I should be bothered is beyond me. Another phone call is received from the neighbour telling me that the water is now halfway up the wall and entering the house. I phone Spencer again and he says that he is on his way.

Passing through Valbonne the next day, we visit some friends who were our former neighbours. After lunch we decide to take a peek into the courtyard of our old house as I have a nagging worry that Spencer has still not been. I look over the railings; water is flooding into the study and kitchen. I climb over the high spiked fence, slither down the wet wall and then wade through the courtyard to clear the leaves from the drain. Hey Presto! The water quickly disappears. Having not heard any news from Spencer, I call him the following day.

"Hello mate" is his usual greeting when he finally answers the phone. *"You wouldn't believe it, but I had a bloody nightmare yesterday. Tried to get up there, but couldn't make it to the end of the road! Trees uprooted everywhere. Flood water turned Valbonne into Niagara Falls. The police blocked all roads and I had to turn back. I will pop up there later and take a look once they have cleared the trees."*

I say nothing – funny how we drove in and out with no problem.

Phone calls from Spencer are commonplace, asking questions that could easily be answered if he could find the manual that he lost within the first week. It is a feeling of guilt that keeps me answering his questions, as I was the one who recommended him. Twelve months have passed since we sold the house but still I receive calls.

On holiday in New York, we are just about to step onto the Empire State viewing platform when my mobile rings.

"Hello mate," says Spencer. *"that ring tone sounds like you're abroad?"*

"I'm on holiday in New York," I say.

"How lovely. Anyway, I won't keep you long. The cleaners say that there is an awful smell of shit in the house. I suspect that the septic tank is blocked. Where's the tank located?"

"There is no tank. As I told you, the house is on mains drains. Somebody has probably shoved something down a toilet. You will have to call out a plumber or get your hand down the U-bend," I tell him.

He lets out a long *"Yeeessss"* which is his code for no fucking chance.

"Tell you what mate, think I'll just leave it and see what happens."

Three days pass. 5am New York time the phone rings.

"Hello mate. Still on holiday?"

I look at my watch, *"Yes I am, and it's very early."*

"Is it really? Sorry about that mate. Anyway, I just wanted to know what you thought the problem could be as there is shit coming in the front door?"

"Probably the fact the toilets are blocked!" I say half asleep.

"Do you know any plumbers?" he asks.

"Not in fucking New York at 5am I don't! Surely as a guardian you must have some numbers? Anyway, I gave you all the tradesmen contact details in the manual," I reply.

"Manual? Don't remember that old chap."

An appropriate moment for me to resign from my role as the guardian's angel.

CHAPTER 17
JE NE COMPRENDS PAS

It seems almost ironic that I have come to live in France, when as a schoolboy I was suspended for a few days because I skipped French lessons. I never sat or passed the exam, thinking at the time that I would have absolutely no use for the language.

Time is precious when living and working in London and with plans to move to France at full steam, the thought of attending night-school to learn this beautiful language was always side-stepped with one excuse or another. Besides, Helen already has a language degree in French and German so I can rely on *Madame Google* for all interpreting.

In London, social gatherings with friends need to be planned many weeks in advance. Weekends are the favoured option as the pressure of work and the long hours undertaken by many, mean a mid-week gathering will start late and finish early. Social diaries need to be referred to on several occasions and brief text messages send nothing more than a calendar date followed by a question mark until a suitable time is agreed by all parties.

In France, we do not find this a problem as events are thrown together at the last minute and phone calls with open invitations are the normal practice. Soon, regular *faces* become friends and conversations rarely focus on house prices or work as many in this region have escaped the normal daily grind. People prefer to discuss other things, be they simple or profound, just as long as they are interesting. Weather and its effects are still however a common topic of conversation.

Because of the generally warmer weather in the South of France, the climate has the automatic effect that people become a lot more body conscious. Men as well as women think about their own physical appearance and happily discuss their latest diet or skincare routine. It is not unusual for tips to be passed around and results admired by fellow practitioners.

Whilst sitting at a barbeque with a good friend called Paul, who is a bear of man with great style and a personality to match, I make a comment about his brown, sun-kissed legs, my attention drawn to them as we were still in spring. He leans across the table and in a soft voice to avoid others hearing says:-

"I will let you into a little secret. I use fake tan."

"No! Really?" I whisper in reply.

"Yeah, it is really easy. You just buy the spray-can version and hey presto you have this great tan."

We nod conspiratorially at each other as we sit back from the table and Paul raises his finger to his lips in a *hush, keep it to yourself* gesture, which is quickly acknowledged by me running a finger and thumb over my mouth to emulate a *zipper* as I shake my head up and down in agreement. We both tap our noses – *just you and me know*.

Excited by this revelation, I cannot wait to visit our local supermarket and the following day I find the sun care shelf brimming with fake tanning lotions. I decide that I need to buy the darkest one I can find and settle on the *Caribbean Cruise* version. I pop the can into my basket along with other grocery items, so I am not seen as vain by the check-out girl. She passes the items at breakneck speed over a scanner - this indicates the start of our race to see if I can pack my bags quicker than she can push and shove the items down the metallic slipway. To date, I have yet to win.

On returning home, I scan the instructions on the reverse of the canister, but I don't understand a word as they are all in French. I decide that the process cannot be complicated and in my eagerness to emulate Paul, I quickly strip naked in preparation for spraying. I apply a generous coat all over whilst bending legs and stretching arms to reach the reverse side of my body but avoid my face which is naturally bronzed. The vapours are flying around the room like an insecticide spray, making me cough and splutter. I stand and wait for the lotion to dry – I see no difference.

I apply a second, more generous coat and stand in a star shape to allow faster drying of the product. I look in the mirror with disappointment at the results. Maybe I should ask my wife what the instructions say? No - I will surprise her with my new Caribbean holiday colour and wait until I have completed the process.

A further eight coats are applied in quick succession and a complete canister is used. Useless - no change whatsoever!

I am woken early the following morning by Helen,

"WHAT on earth have you been doing?" she asks in a tone reserved for those times when she already knows the answer.

I raise the bed sheet which by now resembles the Turin Shroud and look at my naked body which is glowing bright orange. I climb from the bed and look in the mirror at a body covered in orange streaks that have no boundaries. My toenails are orange, the soles of my feet are orange and even my testicles and penis look like they have been dipped in luminous, possibly radioactive, body paint. Looking at the colour of my penis, which by now is reminiscent in colour of a chorizo sausage, I thank my lucky stars that I had not sprayed my face. It would be many weeks before the luminosity subsides.

I telephone Paul to complain about his tanning secret but he can do little more than laugh at my predicament. I am thankful that I never followed his advice on how to check for an enlarged prostate gland!

My lack of ability to read French is compounded by my poor spoken French and on several occasions this has created problems - and unnecessary expense - much to the frustration of my wife. The gay gardener, Noel, is a tall and strapping man with a muscular physique required for gardening but also much admired by his male friends. He is a lovely chap who is always accommodating and nothing is too much trouble. He is very talkative and enjoys the long early morning conversations with Helen who struggles to function much before 9 o'clock.

Noel will often talk to me and although I have difficulty understanding his accent, I am polite enough to nod and say *yes* in French even when I don't understand. I have learned this trick as I have noticed a pattern to his conversations with Helen where she does lots of nodding at the start of a discussion, a few *"ouis"* every now and again and then the French shake of the head with lots of *"non, non, nons"* with *"tutting"* in-between. This rhythm is adopted for our conversation and seems to satisfy Noel who is of the opinion that I have obviously understood everything, when in reality I have understood nothing whatsoever. Never mind, this pattern seems to work for us too.

Helen is out for most of the day, at her painting group that meets every Tuesday on the outskirts of Valbonne. Although she is an excellent artist and has her own studio at home, it is the social element that she enjoys and the routine of meeting friends with similar interests.

"Coo Coo" shouts Noel, which announces his arrival.

"Coo Coo, Noel" is always my response.

Lots of talking from Noel starts the instant I am locked into his visual field and as per normal I follow the pattern, nodding and agreeing until the point where I think I should be *tutting* and saying *non* - but today we do not get that far.

"*OK*" Noel says with a large smile as he walks off.

Several hours pass as I work on another business idea in my small office when I hear the door open and Helen entering the hall.

"Hello" I shout from my office.

"What the bloody hell is going on?" she responds in anger.

I stop my work and walk down the turreted stairwell. What is she so angry about?

"Have you seen the garden? Three green lawns have been completely turned over by Noel and his digging machine. Why is he doing that?

"He must have gone mad. There was nothing wrong with those lawns apart from a few weeds" I reply.

Helen storms out into the garden and I watch as lots of conversation and gesturing of arms takes place with Noel. She slaps her forehead as if to indicate idiocy and then stomps back to the house.

"By all accounts," she starts *"he had a long conversation this morning with SOMEONE about the weed-infested lawns and during this discussion it was agreed that he should tear them up and lay new ones!*

I fidget.

"Who would have said such a stupid thing?" I ask fearing I know the answer.

"You did!" she said as her finger jabbed the air.

From this moment I am banned from ever discussing with Noel what work needs to be completed. To ensure we have both understood, Helen makes us stand in the kitchen whilst she explains to Noel, in French, that he is never to take direction from me again. At least I think that is the conversation? I do pick up on a couple of words like *idiot* and *stupid* which Noel seems to take very well as he smiles a lot. At least I think they are directed at Noel?

Perhaps now is the right time to learn French.

CHAPTER 18

FRENCH PLUMBING

Although a little unsavoury, I feel that a chapter concerning plumbing may be essential for those people who are considering moving to France on either a permanent or semi-permanent basis. During the time my wife and I were making plans for moving to France, we devoured any book that talked of the magical Riviera, while many wet Sunday afternoons were spent watching the film *To Catch a Thief*. Everything was viewed through rose-tinted spectacles. But to get a true flavour of life in the South of France you need to take off the glasses - I guarantee that you will think of me when you have blocked toilets – because it *will* happen!

For those familiar with the reliable and efficient plumbing of England, it is always a shock when a dream home, at times costing millions, has poor sanitation. Despite a certificate of conformity issued by an official inspector, this is no guarantee that anything actually works. The appointed agent has a tick sheet and for questions concerning plumbing these are simply answered by pouring a brightly coloured dye down a toilet or sink while the inspection hatches, located somewhere in the undergrowth, are removed as they wait patiently for the coloured water to appear. Once seen, this is the green light to issue the important, but useless, document.

It is a hot day and the sun had risen early, heating the ground. We have moved into our *latest* dream home and renovation work is complete, apart from the issue of the toilet system being connected to the hot water feed by an incompetent plumber. We know this can be resolved when time allows but for now we have to live with the problem that each time the toilet is flushed, hot water enters the pan and creates a sauna. Our backsides are slowly cooked by steam rising from the porcelain bowl. A note pinned to the wall is sufficient warning to guests of potential scalding from the toilet seat with a gentle reminder to wipe condensation from warm arses before departing.

Helen has left the house early to meet a couple who have employed her to re-design their newly purchased villa. They are interested in seeing further examples of her work so she invites them to our home for a light lunch. All I am required to do is rustle up a chicken salad and ensure the house remains tidy, but much more importantly, I need to look smart, with a clean shirt and brushed hair, and then play the part of a successful interior designer's husband.

Sinks are wiped and several flushes of the toilet to wash away the bleach do no more than fill the bowl to its brim and steam up my glasses. A smell of sewage starts creeping over the house. The toilet gurgles like a geezer warning of impending eruption and I am concerned that a problem is going to arise in the middle of the *Very Important Lunch*.

I quickly phone my brother-in-law and ask him to come over to the house and assist me in locating the problem. Time is slipping away fast and my thought is that two heads would be better than one. I change clothes ready for the journey into the *vide sanitaire*, a sort of cellar area under the house while Phil takes up his position next to the vent and inspection covers located outside of the house.

The ceiling to the *vide sanitaire* is low and the damp ground from the previous week's rain has made the area slightly moist and slippery. At least I hope it was the rain! Fortunately the sewage pipes are visible so no removing of floorboards or tiles is required. The descent angle of the pipes is minimal, as per normal in French houses, but I notice that the exit point pipe has an elbow joint going up. No wonder the pipes are backing up. This would need looking at very soon, but for today we decide that blasting with water will help move *things* along as a temporary measure.

On tapping the pipes they sound solid, as if filled with concrete and I hope that pushing a hosepipe into them will clear the problem. We suspect that there is probably a minor blockage somewhere.

Phil is complaining about the sewage smell emanating from the ventilation grill. This is nothing compared to the stench I am experiencing underground!

"Can you see anything?" he shouts at me through the vent.

"No," I reply *"Except there is an inspection cap. Maybe I should put the hose in there?"*

The hosepipe is fed through the vent by my complaining apprentice, mumbling that he feels nauseous with the smell. I pull the hosepipe through and coil it nearby.

With both hands, I grip the inspection cap which needs to be turned anti-clockwise several times. It is stiff and my white knuckles indicate the pressure needed to release the cover. I lean towards the outlet at chest height with arms held into my body to give me extra leverage and try again. The cap creaks, cracks and moves slightly. I adjust my hands and grip harder as I turn the cap a bit further than before. It now starts to turn with relative ease and almost pushes itself out. I continue turning the screw cap with one hand and I am delighted that the job does not require a tool bag full of equipment to release the inspection cover.

However, just as I am reaching the last few turns, the cap suddenly flies off, missing my face by inches, rapidly followed by a torrent of excrement and urine. In horror, I try and move my face away from the projectile tube as its cargo pours over my body. I use both hands to try and stop the flow but this has the effect of now spraying the river of brown in every direction. I feel like Red Adair - the famed American oil-well fire-fighter – as I try to cap the flow. The stench is overpowering and my clothes are saturated, but warm because of the wrongly connected toilet.

I hear Phil vomiting as the smell intensifies and the continual slopping noise of excrement hitting the ground adds to his disgust.

Eventually the river runs dry and I am left covered from head to toe in stinking slurry, but my hands stay over the outlet hole just in case a last blast is headed my way. Time is against me and Helen and her clients will be home soon, so I decide that I all I can do is simply screw the cap back on and leave it until later in the day when I can get hold of a plumber.

I crawl in saturated clothing through the *vide sanitaire* and shout at Phil to get a plastic bin bag so I can dispose of my garments. He runs round to the exit door with a bag held at arm's length in one hand and a hosepipe in the other. I strip naked and he sprays me down, all the time complaining of the smell but stopping every few seconds as he retches – but is never quite sick.

Clothes are thrown into the bag and placed in the dustbin as he departs with haste whilst continuing to retch and cough.

I quickly shower and dress, smother myself in aftershave, run my fingers through my wet hair and then rush to the kitchen to prepare lunch for our guests. I have scrubbed my hands raw to ensure I don't poison them and on my wife's return everything looks normal.

She passes me in the kitchen with a whispered comment.

"For god's sake you COULD have brushed your hair!"

"I have been a bit busy," I snarl back through gritted teeth.

Lunch passes with lots of polite conversation but I spend the entire time pushing food around my plate. For some reason I have no appetite.

The following day, a proper inspection by a qualified plumber resolves the problem. It has been caused by tree roots growing into a broken pipe and this was further compounded by the exit pipe going uphill. He confirms that this must have been obvious to the previous owners but they had done nothing to rectify the situation. Both the plumber and I are unsure what actions they took when the blockage caused a problem before, as this must have happened regularly.

Each successive house owned by us has had issues with toilets and plumbing but thankfully none have been as distasteful as this episode. My advice is to check the plumbing before you buy.

Helen often quotes that I am never happier than when I am up to my neck in *shit* - an unfair opinion, as it is due to necessity rather than to any kind of perverse obsession with *merde!*

CHAPTER 19
THE CAP FITS

Although a frustration through life, we have now come to accept and celebrate the fact that we are different from most people. We never truly fitted into corporate life or with the many friends we had in England. It was not a personal difference *per se*, it was the social elements that made us feel excluded: children, work, and the fact that we did not share the desire of others to settle – we never will. With this acceptance, comes the break from long standing friendships that may have survived due to a shared history but over life's journey has seen both parties differ to the point that we probably wouldn't connect if we met now.

In France, we find a common bond with other *étrangers*, the shared desire to do something different through choice and not because of an overseas posting by a large conglomerate.

Moving on from some of our old friends in the UK allows us time to nurture and grow new friendships with people who, it appears, are equally different and who have also come to the opinion that there must be more to life than the accepted blueprint laid down by society. As well as enjoying bonds of deep and lasting friendships, we are always open to new relationships, which can sometimes be transient as people make the South of France their home for a short period of time. But then life is about moments so why not enjoy it whilst you can with whomever you can? *Carpe diem.*

Of course there is always a hedonistic element wherever one goes in the world and some see the South of France as one long party scene. The French Riviera has always attracted the glamorous party people from Scott Fitzgerald to Edward and Mrs. Simpson and finally to the *new blings-on-the-block*. However, one cannot sustain such a lifestyle unless you want to end up looking like Keith Richard's grandpa!

We now have an extensive rainbow of friends and do not feel shoehorned into any one particular group. We like the eclectic mix of nationalities and personalities which makes for very lively and interesting conversations and general *bloody good times* without the competitive London element of keeping up with the Joneses. To detail them here without tripling the size of this book is impossible. Perhaps if a second book is written, I can expand on some of the wonderful characters we have met and come to love.

Although we have found a large degree of contentment we remain ever restless and continue to discuss our next adventure. But for now we have found a cap that fits.

Five years of living in France have passed very quickly. It would have been easy to stay in the rat race, earn lots of money and fritter it on items to give one a feel-good factor for a few hours. It takes real effort to step off the treadmill and start a new life, and even more effort to stay off, but once the leap has been made, there are many advantages to be had. We are all programmed to bemoan our lot, but the reality is that I dance to no one else's tune and wish never to return to corporate life. With a wife who speaks fluent French and with mine just above incompetent, we will remain as we are while the sun still shines, and gloat at the weather reports from England.

I shall stay in France as long as possible, but may return to England one day - when old and grey. My *Franglais* will improve little until it ceases to provide such a source of amusement for the locals.

Despite riding a roller-coaster of financial ups and downs, we now have the ability to generate sufficient money to live comfortably. We have broken the chains that kept us locked to a desk for years. We have swapped a lifestyle perceived to be successful and are now content with simple experiences such as sitting with our toes in the sand and watching the mountains change colour as the sun sets.

For a while, I went backwards and lost an element of self-respect and self-worth. When nobody is your master and what is seen as social status has gone, no structure exists to the day, week, month or year. I lost sight of who I was, my hair grew long, shaving was an irregular occurrence and lethargy was my constant companion. But a simple routine, such as walking the dog and having time to look at the world around me, kick-started the new era in my life.

Maybe Aristotle was right, we should have goals, for without them there would be no journey. The end of the rainbow merely represents our own desires and aspirations which should inspire us to continue on life's path. This realisation must not stop us following our dreams and taking a leap in the direction we think is right. If you risk nothing, you end up risking everything, because one day Aristotle's rainbow's end will punch us from life.

What I have now come to accept is that I shall never be poor as long as I have freedom, I shall never be unhappy now that I have choice and that monotony is the only reward of the cautious.

TO BE CONTINUED...

SHOPDROPPING

Shopdropping - The *modus operandi* of entering a well-established store or library and leaving a book on the shelves – i.e. **shoplifting in reverse**.

Anybody who finds a copy and enjoys the read, PLEASE purchase a second copy and shopdrop them back into circulation. Thank you for your support – you are now "*A.Somebody!*" and helping in making this book viral.

If you are worried about shopdropping then why not leave a copy on a bus, plane, train or tube? At the very least walk up to *A.Somebody* new and give them a book explaining why you are doing so.

But of course you could just buy the book, keep it and enjoy it again in the future.

Happy shopdropping!

ABOUT THE AUTHOR

I have not given my name as *I think* it is unimportant to my story. But if you decide you want to know who I am and possibly put a face to a name, then the clues are there. Use the information gleaned from this book and the internet should eventually uncover my identity.

I will be happy to answer any questions you may have and will enjoy hearing your thoughts about my book. Should you wish to write your own autobiography under this title then please contact me.

I wish you every success in your own life and truly hope that I have not offended anybody with my views and opinions. We are all different and if you are content with your chosen life, whatever that may be, then I applaud you – if not, what's stopping *you* changing?

Yours.

A. ~~NOBODY~~
Somebody

Email: theautobiographyofasomebody@gmail.com

Made in the USA
Charleston, SC
21 November 2012